From Outrageous to Inspired

David Hagstrom

Foreword by Roland S. Barth

From Outrageous
to Inspired

How to Build a Community of Leaders
in Our Schools

JOSSEY-BASS
A Wiley Company
www.josseybass.com

Published by Jossey-Bass
A Wiley Imprint
989 Market Street, San Francisco, CA 94103-1741   www.josseybass.com

Credits are on page 181.

Jossey-Bass books and products are available through most bookstores. To contact Jossey-Bass directly call our Customer Care Department within the U.S. at 800-956-7739, outside the U.S. at 317-572-3986, or fax 317-572-4002.

Jossey-Bass also publishes its books in a variety of electronic formats. Some content that appears in print may not be available in electronic books.

Library of Congress Cataloging-in-Publication Data

Hagstrom, David.
  From outrageous to inspired : how to build a community of leaders in our schools / David Hagstrom ; foreword by Roland S. Barth. —1st ed.
    p. cm. — (The Jossey-Bass education series)
Includes bibliographical references and index.
  ISBN 0-7879-7066-2 (alk. paper)
  1. Elementary school principals—Alaska—Fairbanks—Case studies. 2. Community and school—Alaska—Fairbanks—Case studies. 3. School improvement programs—Alaska—Fairbanks—Case studies. 4. Educational leadership—Alaska—Fairbanks—Case studies. 5. Denali Elementary School (Fairbanks, Alaska) I. Title. II. Series.
  LB2831.924.A43H33 2004
  372.12'012—dc22   2003023723

Printed in the United States of America
FIRST EDITION
HB Printing   10 9 8 7 6 5 4 3 2 1

The Jossey-Bass Education Series

Contents

Foreword

Along the coast of Maine, at the edge of Johns Bay, lies an unusual saltwater passage. Narrow and tortuous, it meanders through a formidable maze of rocks and ledges and islands. Yet as long as one does not deviate far from its center, this passage offers remarkably deep water, deep enough for safe navigation of even large vessels. The passage is duly noted on the chart as "Thread of Life."

I find that this tidy little volume you are about to read evokes for me the Thread of Life. It is indeed David Hagstrom's story of traversing impediments, dangers, and threats—all while staying centered, searching for, and usually finding the depths of life.

I have known David for a quarter of a century. I've joined him in settings as varied as Sitka, English Bay, and Fairbanks in Alaska; the coast of Maine; Harvard University; a hospital in Evanston, Illinois; and along the Willamette River beside Portland and at his cabin in central Oregon.

The fathoms that have kept him buoyant for close to seven decades are captured for me within these pages by several consequential words: influence, vision, spirit, community, and heart. Let me say a word about each.

Influence: David is a humble person. He says that the remarkable successes he has witnessed have been at the hands of others. "Learning communities build themselves," and "the group becomes the leader," he tells us. Yet he understates his part. He shuns the label "leader" and surely does not suffer "leadership bullies"—those leaders who believe they know it all. Yet he exerts leadership in his own powerful and idiosyncratic ways. If not a leader, call him then a coach, a team builder, a servant leader, a visionary, an enabler, a community builder, an activist, a revolutionary.

The story of the remarkable transformation of Denali Elementary School in Fairbanks, Alaska, which follows, is testimony to David Hagstrom's remarkable capacity to influence teachers, students, parents, a school, and an entire community. With his words here, his sphere of influence extends still further.

Vision: "A people without a vision shall perish"; so we learn in the biblical book of Proverbs. As well, a school without a vision and an educator without a vision shall perish. This is why so many schools and educators are at risk these days. As you will see, the vision David developed with the Denali school community is a majestic, soaring, ambitious, optimistic, and demanding vision.

He always holds before him the lamp that illuminates his vision—for himself and for the rest of us. By doing so, he challenges each of us to craft our own vision, exhorting us always to keep our visions before us, where they may enlighten our work as educators.

Spirit: Every educator is given an opportunity to influence the learning of other human beings—students, their parents, and colleagues. This, if it is done honestly and earnestly, is indeed, as David suggests, a calling, not a job.

The stories that follow are deeply moving, instructional, and spiritual narratives. By asking the question "What do you want for your children here at Denali School?" and by listening, by honoring the responses, and by celebrating the work, David models for us the leader of the spirit and the spiritual leader.

Community: A community is a place full of youngsters and adults who care about, look after, and root for the success of one another and who work together for the good of the whole in times of need as well as times of celebration. This little volume gives new meaning and weight to the concept of a school as a community of learners and a community of leaders.

As if constructing a community was not an ambitious enough lesson plan, constructing a community of learners and leaders is much more so. Building a school culture that is hospitable to profound levels of human learning and leading is the work of David Hagstrom's life—and of this book. He becomes for us nothing less than the chief architect among many architects and the principal teacher of principals of a remarkable community of leaders and learners.

Heart: The stories that follow will make your heart sing as they have mine. What a moving melody! By speaking from the heart, by providing an alternative approach to school reform, David Hagstrom attracts and promotes life-altering events for himself and for the rest of us. And the process of school improvement takes on a life of its own. Whether the harsh, resistant world will ever be ready for David's gentle, revolutionary approach to life and to school improvement is by no means certain. But if they ignore the heart, those who would reform our schools proceed at their own risk.

These, then, are the words and the meanings that spring forth from these pages for me. These are the threads of life for David Hagstrom. These messages are at the center of the channel offering a deep and safe course through the rocky impediments out there.

"Honor the people," David tells us. Well, I am honored to be a part of David's story. You will be, too.

Head Tide, Maine   ROLAND S. BARTH
February 2004

For a new generation of school leaders

Preface

This book challenges educators to think differently about the relationship of schools and communities. Instead of suggesting ways that school leaders might realize greater support from the community surrounding the school, the stories shared here describe a school that, itself, became a community, including its parents and families. (Throughout this book, I use the term *parents* to refer to parents, guardians, and extended family, whether biologically related or not, who care for children.) This book advises principals *not* to set out on a mission of creating community or implementing their personal vision in their school. Rather, this book proposes that the people associated with the school—teachers, principal, parents, and children, along with neighbors and other community members— can take up leadership together to create a learning community for everyone who cares about the school. The feelings and benefits associated with the establishment of a genuine community then flow naturally from the work of the learning community.

This book is about leadership, learning, extended family, and neighborhood. It promotes the adoption of some very different ways of thinking about parental participation and neighborhood involvement in schools. In the stories that follow, schools are viewed as places where people come together, where they find the vision for their school, and where they determine what it is that they all have to offer to help accomplish the mission that they have, collectively, set for themselves. In the process, everyone in the school community takes on a leadership role.

The fundamental purpose of this book, then, is to stimulate thoughtful, caring leadership in schools; it is meant to serve as a guidebook for school leaders seriously engaged in a journey of school improvement and community building. Our schools urgently need leaders who are strong educators *and* community builders. Such school leaders must be able to gather all the people who care about the school, and they must honor them. They need to call forth people's life stories, gifts, and talents; these stories, gifts, and talents will actually create the community—one that is better able to meet everyone's needs.

I've written this book especially for practicing principals and for those who supervise, prepare, or work with principals. Similarly, prospective principals should find this book a realistic, challenging treatment of issues that they will face from day one on the job. This book is also purposefully directed to a new generation of school leaders, since they are our hope for bringing about meaningful school reform. I will be thrilled if teachers and parents also engage with my stories and thinking.

Finally, the stories in this book and my reflections on them provide an elegantly simple framework—rather than a list of dos and don'ts or a recipe—for creatively dealing with the social transformation of recent decades while using a grassroots approach to focus effectively on the central purposes of the school: learning and teaching. Leaders immersed in school change literature know that a blending of top-down and bottom-up activity makes for longer-lasting school change. As I've watched the struggles for school and community reform over these past ten years, I've seen very few examples of grassroots reform efforts. Instead, the nation has become caught up in a frenzy of school reform, resulting in waves of mandated initiatives. However, I've not seen many examples of local communities taking the initiative and creating just the kind of educational program they want for their children. Because of the dearth of accessible examples of grassroots school change, I share these stories with you.

Too often schools and their leaders, reflecting our culture, focus primarily on deficits, and they fall—or are pushed—into scarcity thinking. In these times, which certainly do hold challenges for schools, I offer a book that, at its heart, is a story of abundance.

Enormous Invitations

Meg Wheatley, an organizational consultant, speaks about the "enormous invitation" we have to create organizations that are fully alive. More than a decade ago, I became involved in a life-changing educational adventure at Denali Elementary School in Fairbanks, Alaska, a school that issued an enormous invitation to me. It also grew into a school community that was fully alive. The lives of students, teachers, parents, and neighbors, along with my own life and the life of an entire community, changed because of a simple but profound question I stumbled upon to ask the people whose lives were focused on that school. I was the principal of the school at the time, and the question that I asked them was a basic one: What do you want for your children, here at Denali School?

What evolved is the subject of most of the stories you are about to read. I've told these stories countless times to audiences across the country. Because my life was so extraordinarily changed during my time at Denali Elementary, the stories begged to be told to educators who were wrestling with similar issues of school change and reform. My experiences of bringing about change from within an organization ran counter to what I was hearing and reading about state and national mandates for change and how reform ought to be accomplished.

For a long time, however, I just told these stories. I hadn't thought much about writing them down until I heard Mary Pipher's call for hopeful stories in her book *The Shelter of Each Other*. Here, Pipher writes of the need to rebuild our families and communities by telling hopeful stories. "Everyone has stories to tell. Stories are about imagination and hope. Let's turn off our appliances and invent these stories. Quilted together, these stories will shelter us all" (Pipher, 1996, p. 271).

I was awakened by the call for stories in her book, but I was urged to actually do the writing when Mary Pipher came to Portland, Oregon, in September 1997. Listening intently as Pipher addressed an audience of teachers, counselors, and social workers, I began to hear her particular enormous invitation much more strongly. She told us: "The new millennium will be about restoring community and rebuilding the infrastructure of families. As we prepare for the future, we must tell those hopeful stories of exciting community adventures and of the different ways that people are defining the nature of a family unit."

That was the turning point for me. I set aside the self-doubt and questions that had prevented me from writing the stories: Would there be an audience of educators and parents who would relate and respond to these stories? Would the Denali stories truly encourage other parents and teachers to get grassroots efforts started at their schools? Or would my writing the stories and publishing them be no more than an act of personal aggrandizement? I decided, with Mary Pipher's encouragement (in a personal letter), to write these stories.

In addition, I attended a book talk by Judith Barrington on memoir in which she asked the audience, whether there might be an important theme in each of our lives about which we felt passionate and which, unless we illustrated it with our appropriate stories, would remain unknown in the world. In a conversation afterward, Barrington told me, "Believe that your task is to share with other principals what they would not have known without you."

Finally, a couple of years ago, one of my students at Lewis & Clark College, Donna Dennison, presented me with a gift, a beautiful journal book. Inside the front cover, she wrote this inscription: "David, you have certainly validated what Sam Keen says: 'To be a person is to have a story worth telling. We become grounded in the present when we color in the outlines of the past and the future.' Thank you for encouraging my story and my future." At that point, I realized that there was an important theme in my life about which I felt passionate, and that theme was "Honor the People; It's the Leader's Work." Furthermore, I realized that my students at Lewis & Clark College—school leaders like Donna Dennison— might be able to take my stories and place them next to their own stories of life within a school and find the reading experience both helpful and encouraging. While they may not know it, Mary Pipher, Judith Barrington, and Donna Dennison all extended an enormous invitation to me, which I here accept.

By sharing these stories, based on my experience, I want to extend an enormous invitation to you, too, to help create a school community and a school that is fully alive. In the process, you may become more fully alive as well.

Truth and Story

My use of the story form to tell you about my school leadership experience in Alaska and to share with you how a community of leaders can be built is a conscious one. Let me explain—how else?—by telling the following Hebrew teaching story:

Truth and Story were twins who lived together in the same house in the same village for fifty years. They were much loved in their community and went together every night to visit all their neighbors. Story dressed elaborately for the visits, almost in costumes. She wore elegant robes; strings of seashells, pearls, or glass beads; garlands of flowers; fanciful wigs; and crowns or hats. Every night Story looked a bit different but always intriguing. Truth never wore clothes at all. When they made their rounds each night, everyone they visited embraced Story warmly and greeted Truth more distantly but with great respect. One night, Story was too ill to make the traditional visit, so Truth went without her. The visits lacked the joy and warmth that they had had when Story went along. After several nights of visiting alone and feeling bereft without Story, Truth decided to comfort herself by making the visit dressed in some of Story's finery. That night, wherever Truth went, she was greeted with great hospitality and warmly embraced, for as you can see, Truth dressed as Story is easier to embrace.

Truth dressed as Story is easier to embrace—and stories inspire. As their imaginations are engaged, listeners and readers envision how they might take elements of the story and make them their own. Stories allow listeners and readers room to make of the recollected events what they will, according to their own situation and perspective. I invite you to do just that with these Denali stories.

These stories are based primarily on my memory and on notes from my time at Denali Elementary. From my perspective, I've been as faithful to truth as I can be, but I've heard it said that memory can be rather tricky. Memory may remember the good, yet not the difficult. Memory recalls what it will because strong emotion attaches itself to particular events or to discomforting episodes that we struggle to understand. Then, too, over time, a person selectively remembers; I'm quite sure that's happened with me and with the stories I will tell you here, because I've focused on the most important events in my mind. Perhaps I've magnified situations over the span of years. Maybe my wishes for what could have been have slipped into the actual episodes.

In this book, I often write using the voices of participants in dialogue. While those exact words may not have been precisely spoken, I've made every effort to be faithful to interactions and conversations, to the unfolding events I describe, and to my experience of them. Naturally, someone else might have experienced the events differently, creating a different version of the story or even a different story. Perhaps people of the Denali school community who read this book may remember these things differently, but this is my experience of the endeavor. So my stories and interpretations can also be seen as a kind of memoir. As you read, I ask that you open yourself to this story, to my interpretation of it, and to my memoir, understanding that I am not reporting a research study.

All names and identifying information of persons from my time in Alaska—including teachers and staff at the school, parents, students associated with Denali Elementary, personnel of the Fairbanks North Star Borough School District, and the University of Alaska Fairbanks—have been changed to pseudonyms. The names of persons from my personal past and those of public figures in the educational, literary, and spiritual realms are their own.

Variations on a Theme

This is a book about how to create a community of leaders in our schools—both leaders who are the expected leaders (principals) and leaders who might not be expected (teachers, parents, neighbors, and other community members). It also tells stories about the communities in which principals live their professional lives. While most of the stories relate to the development of the Denali school community (Parts One and Two of the book), some of the stories also relate to the communities in which school leaders are prepared, sustained, or renewed (Part Three).

More specifically, here's the way I've sequenced the stories and my reflections on them: The stories in Part One, about the Denali Project, recount my days as principal at the school; they stand on their own. Part Two elaborates on how I interpret these stories and relate them to the phenomena of community development, school change, and leadership. In Part Three, I offer a set of stories that situate the Denali story and the sense I've made of it in the broader context of my professional and personal life. Finally, Part Four brings together the book's ideas and invites all school leaders to make a difference in their world.

The design of the book allows you to read these parts in order. Some readers may find that each part can stand on its own, and certainly many of the individual chapters can be read singularly.

Instructors using the book with practicing school leaders and principals-in-preparation can employ this book as case material in the following ways: First, have principals or students read the stories in Part One solely. Follow the reading with a discussion centered on the following questions: What are the central issues or problems here? What do you see happening? What are the perspectives of the various groups and individuals in this case? What assumptions and beliefs about leadership do you think this principal lives by? How is this situation similar to and different from your own?

Then have the students read Part Two only, following again with discussion of such questions as the following: What have you learned about this principal's views on leadership? How does he view the relationship of schools and communities? What's your own view of the leader's role in a school? Finally, have the class read Parts Three and Four in tandem, reflecting on these questions: What are the influences in your own life that shape your views and practices of leadership and community development? What experiences, environments, and people have significantly shaped and sustained your views and practices of leadership and community development?

On to the Stories

This book is a set of stories that encompass the school's story and my own. The story is my "true song"; it's the way I am and the way I want to be. Without much doubt, the story articulates an approach I believe holds value for all schools and their leaders. I hope that readers will find it compelling reading as well as a call to find a sense of deeper meaning in their lives as educators. Perhaps some people will see the ways in which I describe bringing about school and community change as simply outrageous, while others might view them as inspired. However you characterize them, I hope that my stories will help you build a community of leaders in your school.

Sisters, Oregon   DAVID HAGSTROM
February 2004

Gratitudes

I know that I was presented with a precious gift when I stumbled into the midst of the "Denali family"—those teachers and staff, parents and families, children, neighborhood folks, University of Alaska Fairbanks partners and professors, and school district leaders that constituted and supported Denali Elementary School. I'll be forever grateful that you took me in.

For the opportunity to write this book, I owe so much to so many, especially those persons who believed in me and the power of these stories during an extraordinarily long literary gestation period. To Richard Ackerman, Roland Barth, Gordon Donaldson, Kim Stafford, and Becky van der Bogert, I offer my deep appreciation for your never-failing encouragement. To my students and colleagues at Lewis & Clark College, I offer my gratitude for your willingness to listen to and read these stories what may have seemed to you endless times. To those who read parts of this manuscript (especially Yvonne Curtis, Caryl Hurtig-Casbon, Ruth Shagoury Hubbard, Rick Jackson, and Parker Palmer), I thank you for your helpful suggestions. To Lesley Iura and the editorial staff at Jossey-Bass, I want you to know that I feel honored that you elected to share my words with a wider audience.

I have been able to write these stories because I belong to a family that strongly values learning and encouraging others. You uphold and inspire me. To you, Karen, the love of my life, who significantly revised this manuscript, generated new text to help me say the things I wanted to say (especially in Part Two), and imagined the way instructors might use this book as case material in their teaching, I say thank you for living with me in the midst of all these stories. I feel such deep gratitude for your belief in me and in this book.

D.H.

The Author

David Hagstrom is a college teacher and storyteller, now living in Oregon. An experienced principal, David's scholarship has focused on the process of transforming schools into authentic communities. He graduated from Grinnell College with a major in sociology, earned a master's degree focused on U.S. history and education from Harvard University, and holds a Doctor of Education in school leadership from the University of Illinois. Over the forty-five years of his educational career, David's work has been relatively equally divided between service in the public schools as a teacher, principal, and central office administrator and service in university departments of educational leadership. This book is primarily the account of his experience as principal at the Denali Elementary School in Fairbanks, Alaska, during the late 1980s and early 1990s. He can be reached on the Web at www.davidhagstrom.com.

Part One

The Denali Story

What happens when a person receives their heart's longing? What happens when a person gets what he says he wants? In my case, after elation came a struggle that required me to let go, listen, and learn. The process of letting go, listening, and learning all began with just one simple but profound question.

The nine stories in this section are all a part of one larger story, a story about my work at Denali Elementary School in Fairbanks, Alaska. It's the story of a school community finding its vision and creating a learning community; it's about building a team of leaders and celebrating the effort. Here, I tell the stories as a narrative and save most of my commentary until Part Two.

In earlier versions of these stories, I referred to them as "stories that make your heart sing." Such stories are ones that resonate at a deeper level than the narrative in words would seem to convey. Some are stories that our intellect may find to be sensible. But because they relate to the human condition, they also evoke our experience and our wise insight about ourselves, the groups we belong to, and the needs of the world. Sometimes these stories don't make sense to our minds, but they bring us to say, "In spite of everything, yes!"

I've heard it said that the future belongs to those who give the next generation a reason to hope. My wish is that these stories might give you a reason to work, with a sense of committed and realistic hope, toward truly good schools that are created by people who take the time to ask one another evocative questions and to build community from the ground up.

Chapter One

Stumbling into the Question

When this story began, I was a professor in the school leadership department at the University of Alaska Fairbanks. It was good and interesting work, especially because it involved visiting teachers and principals in small, so-called bush villages many miles from the university. Traveling on six-seat propeller planes out to "village Alaska" was always an adventure, and once I arrived in the isolated, rural communities, there was always a lot to learn. So life was good.

Finding the Right Fit

And life wasn't good. My work involved serving as a teacher and mentor to school leaders whose daily lives involved life issues and work obstacles that I'd never experienced. While it's true that I'd been an elementary principal in the Midwest in the 1970s, I'd never been a principal in Alaska. Increasingly, I was concerned that I didn't have appropriate and relevant ideas or information to pass along to my students. I worried, thinking they'd write me off as a "know-nothing college professor," just a hurdle to be jumped as they checked off the classes needed for their administrative license.

So at every opportunity, I began to beg for what I called "a substitute experience." While attending statewide educational conferences, I'd butt into the conversations that superintendents were having with what became my standard line: "If you ever need a substitute principal, let's say for six weeks or so, please give me a call. If someone is out on maternity leave or called back home, please don't hesitate to call on me. I need the experience."

The superintendents responded politely, but I never received a call. I think they thought I was simply wanting a "village adventure"— something that would put more vitality into my college lectures. And perhaps that might have been part of my motivation.

At any rate, no one called. So I put that dream to bed and went about my university work. Since getting firsthand experience of the type I desired seemed to be out of the picture, I tried to figure out how I could contribute to what was going on in the public schools of Alaska, from my position as a university-based educator. Perhaps I could share research findings. Perhaps by getting more involved in the work of the schools, even if not as a principal, I'd find a niche that was right for them and right for me. While not what I really wanted, it would be a step in the right direction. So I began attending as many public school meetings as I could, with the intent of finding the right fit.

Until We Can Find a Real Principal

In late August 1988, as a university person attempting to find my niche, I was sitting at a table in the back of a middle school in Fairbanks as its new principal greeted her faculty for the first time, saying: "I'm pleased to be with you as we move into this new school year. We're going to have a good school year. However, I begin with one deep regret; I'm really sad that the school I've come from has not yet found a replacement principal. It's a bit unsettling for me that there's no leader at Denali Elementary."

I remember that moment, and it was unsettling for me, too. Denali Elementary, of all schools, deserved a fine leader. Denali Elementary was the original school in town. It had been such a proud place; it had been the center of the community for many years. Its history paralleled the growth of Fairbanks from its beginning as an early gold mining town through its years as a military outpost and then as the commercial center for the Alaskan interior. As the town grew and other schools were built in outlying areas, Denali

Elementary became less the community center and more the place where no one wanted to be. It had become a rather sad, forlorn, and dreary place. Indeed, its early glory days were gone. Its nearest neighbors were the Salvation Army and a house where illegal drugs were sold.

Denali Elementary was the school attended by many Alaska Native children living in Fairbanks. Many of their families moved back and forth from outlying, rural villages, where they hunted and fished for subsistence, to town, where they worked in the cash economy. Denali Elementary was attended by children of military families as well. Noncommissioned officers and enlisted folk as well were told not to bring their families to Fort Wainwright because there was not enough housing on the base. But families came in spite of this directive and often found dilapidated trailers and substandard rentals off the base for the couple of years they'd be in town. Often these families awaited transfer papers promising better times and warmer weather in Georgia or Hawaii.

A shelter for battered women stood just a few blocks away. Mothers and children who called the shelter home also called Denali Elementary their school. But of course they would have preferred to be in safe homes of their own along with schools in a better location rather than the shelter and its neighborhood school. In fact, lots of people who were at Denali Elementary really didn't want to be there. There were twenty other schools in town. Often parents cleverly pretended that their child lived in another part of town so that any other school could be home. As well, many Denali teachers wanted to be at any other school. It just wasn't seen as a great place to be by many teachers and families.

I thought about Denali Elementary as the meeting began. It was sad that they had no principal there. But during the course of that August meeting, I went on to concentrate more on how I might introduce my "college person's point of view" to the Fairbanks North Star Borough School District. On that orientation day, I just sat there at the table at the back of the room.

At the end of the meeting, I went out to my car and drove back to the university. I went up in the elevator, got off at the seventh floor, and moved toward my office door. As I fumbled with my keys in the lock, I could hear the telephone ringing. Upon entering, I picked up the phone, saying, "Good morning, this is David."

"Good morning to you, David," was the reply. Then the caller declared, "I'm calling your bluff." It was Harry Brady, the school district's assistant superintendent, who continued, "You've told us for years that you want to gain some principal experience in Alaska. Well, we're going to give you that experience. I want you to be acting principal at Denali Elementary. You'll be the principal there—until we can find a real principal. So what do you say?"

"I'll do it, Harry!" I said, hanging up the phone.

Then I realized that I already had a job. So I practically ran to the dean's office and announced, "Dean, we have this great opportunity to truly connect with the public schools" (and I went on to explain the situation).

"Great news, David," he said. "Go for it. You certainly won't have to worry about any conflict with what we do here. A principal's job is basically eight in the morning until three in the afternoon, and what we do here is basically four until ten in the evening. So I say, 'Go for it!' This sounds very good all the way around."

I accepted the dean's "Go for it!" almost as would a little boy receiving permission to go outside to play. After all my waiting, what I had wanted for so long was now mine. I was to be the principal of an elementary school (grades K–5) with about thirty staff members and a student body of about four hundred (later to rise to about five hundred during my tenure), of whom at least a third were students of color, representing Alaska Native, African American, Asian American (for example, Filipino), and Hispanic families. Socioeconomically, these families reflected the Fairbanks community but were predominantly working-class folks. Little did I know it at that moment, but bewilderment and exhaustion would soon be mine as well.

I'd forgotten to ask Harry when I needed to report, so I called back. "Well, school starts tomorrow morning, David. Need I say more?"

I said, "No, sounds good to me." And then my head began to spin. I realized in a split second that wanting to do something and knowing how to do it are two completely different things. But I appeared at the school at 7 A.M. the very next day. Very few people there had the slightest clue about either my identity or my assignment. As I think about it now, I see that I was a bit unsure about both of these matters myself.

When I got home at the end of that very long first day, I looked into the mirror and asked myself, "Hey, David, what have you gotten yourself into now?"

"Hey, David, What Have You Gotten Yourself into Now?"

Those first few weeks were some of the most difficult and exhausting weeks of my life. Looking back on it now, it all seems like quite a blur. Generally, teachers at the school wanted to be told what to do. They frequently asked me, "Can I . . . ?" and "Do I have your permission to . . . ?" I was just the acting principal, apparently just taking care of formalities. Still, to be brutally honest, I didn't know what the hell I was doing. I tried to draw on the ideas and strategies that I was teaching in the graduate-level principal licensure courses I taught, ideas and strategies about organizational and fiscal management, as well as curriculum and program development. I wandered around, attempting to look like I was in charge, and gathered an increasingly long list of teacher's questions to which I'd replied, "Sorry, I don't know the answer to that, but I'll find out and get back to you."

I was particularly bewildered during those early days by the gift of a whistle that I received from someone in the central office. "Here you go, David, this will get you going in your new work," the person told me with a sly smile. "You'll really need this whistle at Denali. Carry it wherever you go and all the time." Why on earth did I need a whistle? Was this whistle to define my work?

Not much time had gone by in my new work, but I was beginning to understand experientially what I had known intellectually before—that there was quite a gap between what I'd been teaching in my graduate school courses and real life in an actual Alaskan school setting. At this point, my earlier experience as a principal seemed long ago and far away. In so many instances in my new work, I simply didn't have a clue as to what to do or how to do it. I was truly quite lost and feeling very alone in the work. "Maybe this wasn't all that great an idea after all," I sadly whispered to myself late one afternoon as I closed my office door and prepared to go to my other job at the university.

A Surprising and Simple Question

In the hallway, I spotted Sally, Peter, Carol, and Lois. I was exhausted. What could I have to say to these two parents and two teachers at the end of this excruciatingly long day? Actually stumbling into their midst, I said, "Hi! I've been thinking about something. Mind if I ask you a new-principal type of question?"

Peter replied, "Sure, go ahead."

I blurted out, "What do you want for your children, here at Denali School?"

There was absolute silence for a really long time. So I asked the question again. "What do you want for your children, here at Denali School?" Determined to get some sort of answer, I waited. I waited for what felt like three minutes—an eternity—in the semi-dark dungeon of a hallway that was painted gray, nearly black.

"Well, you know, David," Lois, the mom of a primary-level child, finally murmured, "no one has ever asked us a question like that. As parents, we talk about it at the Safeway and as we watch the kids play hockey, but we've never talked about it at school before."

I was amazed. I was even more amazed when Sally, another parent, proclaimed, "You know, this is a first. We grouse and complain a lot when we see each other in the neighborhood, but I can't remember talking about what we truly want for our kids here in the school. Maybe this is my only chance, so let me tell you this: I want my kids to be just as interested in exploring and learning inside the school as they are outside of it. With the river right here and the woods so close to our house, my kids just love to build forts and run around through the woods, checking things out. They just love Fairbanks and Alaska and this neighborhood. But then they enter this dank, dark place—what a letdown! My kids like the other kids in this neighborhood, but I have to tell you this. I think they hate the school."

The teachers, looking very surprised, then asked, "So what do you want for your kids?"

With a strong hint of annoyance, Lois called out, "Sally told you what we want. We want our children to be explorers *inside* the school. We want them to be 'discovery kids.' We want Denali School to be an exciting place where kids inquire, investigate, and explore."

The hallway conversation went on this way until after dark. Fully energized, we all wanted more talk like this. "What's next? I finally asked us all. "Shall we talk about this at the next PTA meeting?"

They all laughed at what they obviously considered an absurd question. "If you want to drown this idea, David, that's a surefire way."

Embarrassed, I tried again: "So how do we do this? When do we meet?"

Unsuccessfully playing the calendar game for about five minutes ("What about 4 P.M. on Thursday? What about 8 P.M. on Wednesday?") caused Sally to smile and declare, "I've got a deal for you all. Come over to my house for breakfast at 6 A.M. on Tuesday. Is there anyone here with totally urgent business planned for next Tuesday morning at 6 A.M.?" We all laughed and moved toward the parking lot.

On the way to my "night job" at the university late that afternoon, I felt more energy than I'd experienced in six weeks. My
hopes for the school became much more focused. My thoughts
about what I had to offer these people became much clearer. I felt
that the organization that was Denali Elementary School was somehow inviting me to listen to it. I believed that the school was asking me to help it come alive. In my car that afternoon, I talked to
myself, saying something like this: "David, you know how to do
this. You know how to listen to people as they talk about what's important to them. You know how to help this organization determine
what it wants to be. You *are* in the right place at the right time." On
that afternoon, I felt at home in the school—and at home with
myself. For the first time since the start of school, I couldn't wait to
get back to school the next day.

Chapter Two

Finding the Shared Vision

The five of us—two teachers, two parents, and me—met the next Tuesday at Sally's house, and I did listen. I listened deeply. The individuals in this group spoke again about what they wanted for their children.

Tuesday Morning Meetings

At this Tuesday morning meeting, two ideas surfaced. Clearly, the notion that these folks wanted the children to become explorers, even discoverers, was right at the top of the list. Then there was the matter of the Exxon tanker's massive oil spill in Prince William Sound at Valdez. On that morning, there was much talk about how outsiders had raped Alaska. The group was outraged by the recent tragedy. "First it was the gold miners, then the fish and timber people, and then the oil companies. When will we ever learn to truly care for the land?" After about a half hour, it became clear that we wanted our children to learn how to be explorers and to be givers, not takers.

By 7:30 on that Tuesday morning in mid-October of 1988, this little group of five had begun to articulate an agenda for the school's children. The school should encourage children to be discoverers within the building and, in the process, to become givers, not takers. Energized by the dialogue, we asked, "What's next?"

Someone suggested that we meet again, and Sally offered, "Let's each one of us bring someone else to the table. It doesn't matter whether it's a teacher, parent, child, or neighbor. Let's each bring someone and talk seriously again, to see what we find out."

As we parted that morning, Peter spoke for us all as he urged, "We've found something important here. Let's take it to the logical next step next week!" Thus ended our first Tuesday morning meeting. During that time together, the five of us had come to understand that we deeply cared about the school and its children and that we were going to do our best to take the next steps. When we gathered again, five would become ten. We'd continue to listen in on this organization that was our school. We'd see whether what we'd learned on this first Tuesday reflected what others in our community knew and wanted, too.

"So much more than what we've got is possible at Denali," we told ourselves at that first meeting.

"That question of 'What do we want for our children?'" Sally noted later about that first morning meeting, "it's more than a question. It's more like a call, a call to something deeper for us all. Somehow the question is calling us to share so much more of ourselves than would ordinarily be expected in a school situation like this. I'm amazed at how bold folks are about what they want and how outspoken they are about how things are. No punches pulled, that's for sure. Now that's really different! Why is this group so different from the others we've known?"

As the school day ended, I reviewed that first Tuesday morning meeting in my mind: "These folks are really taking the question seriously. I know it's a small group, but isn't it interesting that they seem so united in what they want? It's not going as I had expected. I thought we'd have such a variety, such variation in the ideas about what they wanted. It's like these people are in collusion. No, it's not really collusion; what's happening here has more to do with people being willing to listen to each other. These people really seem to be open to each other." Surely we'd found much more than we'd bargained for when we had stumbled into that "What do we want?" question. It was almost like the school itself was trying to tell us something.

Alaska's Discovery School

The Tuesday morning meetings continued, week after week. The size of the group increased. Soon we were more than fifty persons strong, with teachers making up about 40 percent of the group (not all the teachers were attending yet), and we were still meeting at Sally's house. There were a handful of neighbors who were not otherwise involved in the school, but the majority of participants at this point represented families with children at the school. There were also a few kids. Although the group's size grew week after week, the desire of the group remained the same. Discovering and giving, these were the themes. On about the fifth Tuesday morning, one of the parents said, "I think we've found our vision for Denali School. We want to create a 'Discovery School.' Am I right?" There was no doubt; this parent spoke for all of us. We'd found what was right for our children and the school. But we were woefully unprepared to engage in the creation of a school with discovery and giving at its heart. From our perspective, it was becoming increasingly clear that we were on the road to creating a school with mathematics and science at its center. We'd come to the understanding that if we wanted each of our children to have an explorer's attitude and skills, the disciplines in mathematics and the sciences would be the best path. But we were hardly prepared to teach math or science deeply or as well as would be needed. In its teaching staff, Denali was quite the typical elementary school. Only one of the teachers possessed a background in and an orientation toward the sciences. Most were prepared to be language arts teachers. And I had been a history major!

We'd definitely arrived at a fork in the road. Thinking back on it, I see that it would have been so easy at this point for us to back off, saying, "Let's stick with what we know. It's been an engaging dialogue, but now let's get back to work." But we didn't say that. Instead, one of the teachers asked, "How can we make this happen?" She continued, "This 'Discovery School' idea—it's truly what we're meant to be. I feel it strongly. And, you know, it doesn't bother me that I'm not really prepared to work with the children now in math and science. I'm hopeful that we'll figure out a way to see to it that I get the information I missed earlier in my schooling. I'm really looking forward to becoming a learner again. I'm really looking forward to learning with all of you. We can do this, don't you think?"

Surprisingly, everyone there agreed, "Yes, of course we'll figure it out. Let's get on with whatever's next."

Miracle in the Making

Such encouraging words caused one of the parents to virtually shout, "I think I've got it! We have a world-class science organization—the Geophysical Institute of the University of Alaska—only about three miles from here. I wonder if anyone there would help us out?" After the group considered the idea for a few minutes, someone produced the staff directory from the university and began assigning folks from our group to call professors in the science and math departments, inviting them to be a part of our project. We targeted certain departments at the university, especially the departments of biology, botany, chemistry, and physics and the Geophysical Institute. We decided to initiate the contacts later that morning. We were a bit timid at the outset of these telephone calls but soon found that everyone that we asked responded with either "I'd love to" or "Of course," even after we told them the hour at which we met! Maybe the university folks were intrigued by such an unusual request; maybe this project furnished a breath of fresh air to a professor's stale work life. Whatever their reasons for such willingness to attend a meeting exploring a relationship between our elementary school and a world-class institution of science learning, we were surprised, energized, and all the more certain that we were on the right track. Lois affirmed, "David, you asked just the right question. And our answer just keeps on coming."

At our next Tuesday morning meeting, eight university professors, including a couple of education faculty in addition to the science folks, gathered with us. They asked a lot of questions: What do you need? How can we help out? What do you want us to do? As professors in the sciences concerned with the state of knowledge in the country's general population, they appeared to be thrilled that teachers and families in an elementary school were interested in the same things they were. As a result, they volunteered, for example, to make available to teachers and children facilities not open to the public, such as the Geophysical Institute's permafrost tunnel (a scientific laboratory).

During the next several 6 A.M. meetings, we arranged to have our university partners offer a science and math program for our teachers, on school time. We wanted to hire permanent substitutes for our entire teaching staff each Friday (the same substitute for each teacher each week). At one of our down moments, when we didn't know how we were going to pay for the ambitious tasks we were beginning to undertake, one of our university folks had challenged us by saying, "This stuff you're wanting to do can be paid for with grant monies."

We replied, "We've never written a grant proposal. We can't do this."

Still she urged us, "Sure you can. I'll help you the first time around, then you're on your own. Once you get a sense of what the granting agencies want and how they want it, you'll do great. Once I teach you what I know about the importance of getting supporting testimonials, you'll be in a good position to request what you need."

She was correct. We paid for the substitutes with grant money that we received from the Alaska Department of Education.

With each passing day, I became more mystified about what was happening. Pleased, yes, but mystified as well. There was definite excitement in the air, especially around the Tuesday meetings. Truly, we all felt there was a miracle in the making! I knew this didn't make a lot of sense, but perhaps it had something to do with the words I was astonished, about midway through our process of responding to the "What do we want?" question, to find written on the university's swimming pool wall: "In the purification of motives, luck forms, reality bends, and surely miraculous events will follow."

After noticing these words at the university, I brought them back to the Tuesday group and asked them what they meant. Ann replied: "For us at Denali it means just this: If we're doing stuff for all the right reasons, then full speed ahead. And we are doing all this stuff for all the right reasons! These kids really are explorers, and it really is time to treat the earth right. I think we have a 'predictable miracle' in our midst. We're about to birth a miracle! And I'm thrilled."

Maybe we weren't all quite as thrilled as Ann was, but it seemed to me that we were all pretty much in awe of what was happening. I was noticing that because of the way we'd grounded ourselves in what we wanted for the children, when we asked someone to get involved, they'd always say yes. When we asked for something from the business community or the school district's central office, they always said yes. When I talked with teachers, they were almost always saying yes. We seemed to have our motives figured out.

When Tom Sergiovanni visited Alaska as a conference speaker that year, he also talked with Denali teachers, reminding us that we got yes responses so often because we "inquired together." In other words, at Denali Elementary, the principal didn't merely tell teachers and parents what to think or do, and those parents and teachers didn't merely listen to me as the principal. Instead, as time went on, we asked questions and developed answers together, becoming increasingly free to express ourselves, free to take risks, free to fail. The process of inquiry learning that we were beginning to experience appeared to have cut us loose from the usual bureaucratic boundaries of roles and hierarchies.

All of that was interesting, but I became most fascinated with the fact that, all of a sudden, we seemed to be involved in what we called "collective learning." That, in my opinion, was the miraculous event. As I looked around me, it seemed that most of us as teachers and parents were becoming like eager little kids finding out about the world for the first time. We seemed to be like just so many innocents who'd just landed on Earth. We were curious. We were intrigued. We cared. We were all doing things for the fun of it. In truth, we had created a learning community.

Chapter Three

Learning Anew

After one of our Tuesday morning meetings, I volunteered to ask our students how they felt about Denali Elementary becoming a "Discovery School." Here are a few representative samples of the written responses from some fourth- and fifth-grade students:

> I think the Discovery School idea is a good idea because science and math are fun. I hope to make a career out of science. I know that a lot of the kids in my class love to explore and so do I. I think the teachers should learn more about science so they can share more about that subject. I also think we should learn how to help the environment. [Lucy]

> I'd like the teachers to learn more about science so they can tell the students more about the earth and sea. I like to discover things so I think the Discovery School idea is good. [Billy]

> I think the Discovery School idea is a great idea because it gives the kids a chance to learn what they're interested in. With a Discovery School you can go further than the textbook and do things like planting and growing a garden. It would be neat for the teachers to learn more things to teach us. [Mary]

At our next meeting, I read a couple of the student responses. The notion of our becoming Alaska's Discovery School was now encouraged by the children's positive reactions. Parents and teachers attending that meeting again found themselves deeply involved in conversations about the nature of our children and also about the ways by which we could in fact become a Discovery School. "Our children really are curious," we affirmed.

"They're very interested in animals," said one teacher.

"They love to figure out how things work," said another.

Parents had talked about the connections we could make with the science departments at the high schools and at the university. "We have a world-famous science institute just three miles from here," one parent reminded us again. "Let's continue to push and find out if anyone over there wants to help us." So that meeting ended with us again reaching out for help.

This was the beginning of what became a characteristic action of the Denali Project (as we began to call it): We declared what we didn't know and what we wanted to know. In this case, we didn't really know either the body of knowledge or the methods of science and mathematics. We asked who could help us to obtain what we needed. In this case, we knew that the university had the resources.

After our exploratory meeting with the initial group of university staff, the number of our university colleagues sifted out. We had gained the support of university deans and department heads, the directors of the scientific institutes, and so forth. Now, the persons most keenly interested in the ongoing project, those with the particular expertise we needed, continued to meet with us. Beginning at the next Tuesday meeting, three university science professors and a high school physical science teacher joined our discussions. By now, it was clear that we were accomplishing much more than just identifying the characteristics of the school and determining the kind of schooling we wanted for our children. We were also developing a new understanding of the interests of our children and how they learned. We were beginning to realize the importance of the simple idea of connecting the curriculum to our children's interests. Perhaps of greatest importance was the sense that parents, teachers, and other community members were beginning to feel some ownership in the school. Everyone at the Tuesday morning meetings felt that we were doing something significant. We decided that it was time to begin involving Denali's entire teaching staff.

When all the teachers were invited to the expanded Tuesday sessions, we began to write down our conversations in detail. We heard comments such as the following:

"I've been wondering what you've been up to, and now I'll be able to find out for myself."

"You know, folks have been saying Denali is the best-kept secret in Fairbanks. Maybe the secret has something to do with Tuesday mornings."

"Although 6 A.M. is awfully early, if you're figuring out ways to help the kids, I'll be there."

And so they were. From this time forward, virtually all of the teachers attended our 6 A.M. Tuesday morning meetings. People squished in next to each other on the floor, sat on the stairs, and stood where they could in Sally's split-level house.

Now there was no turning back. We'd found, we believed, the way to turn our school around. That way was to involve the parents, teachers, and members of our wider community in meaningful conversations about our children, how they learned, and what they wanted to learn. Although we were working within the context of the district's traditional curriculum, our desires were still strongly influenced by the characteristics of our children. As a school community, we'd grown a lot. As a school, we'd become a community.

Becoming a Focus School

During the winter, the membership of our Tuesday Morning Club (as we'd begun to call ourselves) decided that the time was right to begin including the school district office. The superintendent had been talking about the availability of funds for the older schools to make physical changes and order new equipment. Because Denali was the oldest elementary school in Fairbanks, we felt it deserved a portion of those monies. Tuesday Morning Club members had visited the newer schools and had seen the modern computer labs and the up-to-date science facilities. They felt that their school should have similar supplies and equipment.

The superintendent and members of the school board were also beginning to talk about the possibility that schools might apply for special "focus program" grants. The superintendent felt strongly that if a school focused on a particular subject area or discipline, that school's program would become more attractive and exciting to children and parents. Denali's Tuesday Morning Club saw these focus program grant possibilities as inviting and intriguing. Why couldn't Denali Elementary be the first focus school in Fairbanks? How could we access such funds? I was instructed by the Tuesday Morning Club to confer with central office personnel to find answers to these questions.

The superintendent informed me that a representative group of parents and teachers from Denali Elementary should make a presentation to the school board to request status as a science-math focus school. But before we gave the presentation to the board, we'd need to practice before the group of central office administrators known as the superintendent's cabinet. The central office staff would let us know if our presentation was ready to be given to the board. We agreed on a time and a place for the practice presentation. Then the superintendent told me, "You'll only have twelve minutes to get your idea across. Board agendas are very full, and that's all the time you'll be given. And remember, the focus programs should forecast long-term effort."

"Twelve minutes is all we've got?" was the response when I told Tuesday Morning Club members of my success.

"Yes, that's what we've got," I said.

"How can we get our vision across within that time frame?" they asked.

Jim, a high school science teacher, stood up and proclaimed, "Our only hope is to make it almost totally visual. The board members will need to see what it is that we have in mind."

The club decided to make seven posters. The person holding the poster would give a very brief explanation; the message would be in the visuals. Each statement would be a poster title. (I suppose that nowadays we would devise a PowerPoint presentation!) Here are the words that we determined best expressed our vision:

- Denali Elementary Wants to Be Alaska's Discovery School
- Total Community Effort
- Teachers as Learners
- A New Partnership with the University
- Curriculum Based on Needs of Our Children and of Alaska
- Bringing About Change from Within
- Shared Leadership

Because our Denali family was such a rich mix of ethnic and racial origins and socioeconomic standings, we decided to have the seven posters held by seven children who represented Denali's special cross section of the world. Our seven adult speakers should represent the makeup of our Tuesday Morning Club, so we selected a high school teacher, a university professor, a member of the Fairbanks business community, the principal (me), a Denali teacher, and two parents to tell our story and to make our case for focus school status. We truly wanted Denali Elementary's focus to be on inquiry in science and mathematics—in other words, we wanted Denali to be what we called a "Discovery School"—and we viewed the board presentation as the critical first step toward the realization of our dream.

On the appointed day, when we made our practice run in front of the superintendents' cabinet, only the superintendent responded. "Twenty minutes long," Dan said. "I told you twelve minutes, and I'm holding you to that. Give it again, and cut out eight minutes. Also, I told you when you gave me the overview that we'd consider this idea only if it was guaranteed to be a long-term effort. I don't want to see you focusing on something else in a couple of years. Let me know the number of years you're going to commit to this idea. I think you should commit to the Discovery School idea for seven years."

We cut those eight minutes by dropping one point from each person's presentation and talking faster. More important, I told the group, "Okay, folks, from this point forward, we've got a seven-year plan." We gave the presentation again. Exactly twelve minutes. When we got to the end, Dan stood up, moved toward the door, and told us, "See you at the board meeting." That was that. We cheered!

As it has turned out, the superintendent's demand that our plan be worked out to cover a period of seven years accounted for much of the success of the endeavor. Dan's insistence that we commit ourselves year after year, without yielding to other inviting projects or interests that tempted us, resulted in an important difference between our project and other innovations that flit in and out of schoolhouse doors. In an exhausting three-week period between the rehearsal and the school board presentation, the members of the presentation team did, in fact, work out a seven-year timetable for staff development, curriculum revision, student development, and community activities.

Our actual presentation was, at one and the same time, a bit anticlimactic and marvelously celebratory. We'd had such fun in the early days of the Denali Project, including hatching the Discovery School idea and learning together from our science partners at the university. Then so much of our energy had gone into creating the presentation, rehearsing before the superintendent and his cabinet, and especially developing the seven-year plan we had envisioned at the superintendent's insistence. After all of that, the school board presentation was over in just twelve minutes! Yet an exhilarating phenomenon also occurred at that meeting. More than one hundred Denali parents crowded into the boardroom. It was standing room only, and according to one board member, more parents and teachers attended our presentation than had attended any other noncontroversial, noncrisis school board activity. I heard one mom exclaim as she left the room, "I'm so proud of Denali tonight." I think that's how we all felt. We'd accomplished something very special in a six-month time period. As one Tuesday Morning Club member expressed later on, "We're such ordinary people, but we've actually accomplished some rather extraordinary things." What these ordinary people did was indeed extraordinary. They turned a school around. In the process, the board had voted to name Denali Elementary a science-math focus school.

Teachers Working Together

Many writers and researchers familiar with teachers and schools say that teachers don't work together and that there's very little sense of collective learning going on in schools. Peter Senge, author of *The Fifth Discipline* and a favorite educator among the Denali staff, suggests to educators that teachers need to learn to work together as teams (O'Neil, 1995). Senge also says that schools are, of course, organizations of learning, but that most are *not* learning organizations. Not so at Denali. What I noticed was that teachers, parents, and community members were definitely engaged in the process of their own learning. What interested me the most was that the inquiry focus seemed to erase bureaucratic boundaries and role differences that could have been obstacles between the teachers and me.

Denali now seemed so different from the other schools I'd known. Teachers seemed so free to learn, so free to take risks, so free to fail, so free to be and express themselves. I began to feel this freedom too. Denali felt different from some other schools, where the principal tells and the teachers listen or where an expert "inservices" and workshop attendees are "in-serviced." The staff was getting genuine dialogue going. There was beginning to be the kind of professional culture that I had yearned for over so many years. I'd always wanted the kind of school that Judith Warren Little, a university educator who writes about the professional culture of schools, describes so invitingly (Little, 1982). She describes schools where teachers observe and talk about their teaching, where teachers prepare teaching materials together—that is, where teachers teach one another the practice of teaching. That's the kind of school I'd always wanted, and that's the kind of school Denali was becoming.

At Denali, over the years of the project, we did establish a strong professional culture. All that Judith Warren Little identifies was present at the school: The teachers constantly talked about their teaching. That was because they were learning something new and were trying to figure out how to share their new understandings with the children. They were in one another's classrooms continually. That's because they were learners finding new ideas and information together, not teachers competing with one another. The teachers often prepared teaching materials together, because the university staff had gotten them started by having them work together on the projects they had been assigned for our Friday School. Denali teachers did, in fact, teach each other the practice of teaching. That's because the art of teaching became important to them. Teacher after teacher told me things like "The thrill I get from teaching well is alive in me again." Often, the teachers who talked in this way would go on to say that they were revisiting the ways they had thought about teaching back in their early days, when they were just getting started.

Like Eager Little Kids Discovering Things for the First Time

In the midst of a science or math class for our staff, I'd look around me. Here were the teachers all right. But they weren't complaining or looking for answers from an "expert" who'd come to fix them. They weren't grumbling about some problem that had occurred at an assembly or on the playground. Rather, they were huddled into groups of three or four, solving a math problem together or focusing on a science experiment they'd devised in order to understand some science phenomenon. They were elated when they found a solution or came up with a new slant on the problem. The teachers were learners again, and they loved this new life. It was as though they'd been untethered from their old ways; there was a look of relaxed freedom on each face. I remember looking over at Christine in the midst of class one day. She looked back at me and said, "Hey, David, isn't this fun? It's like we're kids again."

Our University Teachers

During the course of the Denali Project, many fine university teachers were involved in our work. But one, Alan, became everyone's favorite. Alan, then an instructor in the School of Natural Sciences at the University of Alaska Fairbanks, was a biologist and wildlife expert whose knowledge we drew upon to provide a unique experience for the teachers and for the students. Alan's work with Denali teachers also made it a special and singular experience for him.

How did a scientist training prospective scientists make the shift to working with elementary school teachers wanting to tap the discovery skills of their students? "It was almost a dream come true," Alan answered an interviewer, "but it was happening too early from my perspective" (Lockwood, 1991, p. 11). Alan had thought about doing some science education work with an elementary school, but an invitation like ours came earlier than he had anticipated. We invited Alan and a science educator in the School of Education to provide an overview of what the university could offer the Denali staff. Alan gave the staff something unexpected, instead of what they might have anticipated in terms of a lecture, providing an idea of how he'd work with them in the proposed two-year course.

Alan remembered, "I took in a dead vole, laid it on the table, and asked the teachers if it were alive. Therefore, we began talking about the properties of life by looking at something dead. Next, everyone went outside with simulated dead voles—in this case, pieces of meat. They sat underneath trees or in places where I had placed pieces of meat the day before. I asked them to watch the wasps in the area and ask questions" (Lockwood, 1991, pp. 11–12).

Alan designated one person in each group of four or five to be a scribe who wrote down their questions. Each teacher picked a question they wanted to investigate. They figured out answers to their questions and generated more questions for which they wanted answers, experiencing the scientific method in the process.

The teachers just loved Alan's ways of working with them. They said of his teaching, "He takes us where we're at, he listens to what we need, and he doesn't douse us with a lot of university lecturing."

And Alan always invited the teachers' students into the teachers' learning process. He'd say, "Go back and talk with your students about what you're learning."

The teachers did tell their students about their science class. For instance, whenever Patricia went back to her class and her students would ask, "Hey, what did you learn today?" and she'd tell them, "Hey, I have an assignment due," they'd help her with the assignment.

Jazzy Collaboration

The overall atmosphere that I remember most from those Denali Project times was of everyone working constantly on assignments. We did one project after another, in teams with one another. I don't recall much solo work. Because this was so different from business as usual in typical elementary schools, we'd talk about our ways of being with one another. We'd comment about the mentality that exists in most schools, where the teachers' main ways of thinking were from the perspective of their "side-by-side caves." Teaching can be so individualistic; often you're so much on your own. And many like it that way. It's true; it pleases many teachers that their classroom is their own world, just as many principals enjoy work in "their" building. It's almost as though there are signs outside classroom doors that read "Colleagues, Stay Away. Trespass at your own risk. I'm on my own in here, and I like it this way." Teachers are often good about advocating cooperative learning for their kids, but the adult version of the same is often quite distasteful to them. Because it was so with many teachers, we wondered what made the difference here and why were we were becoming comfortable with a collaborative team approach.

Perhaps Wynton Marsalis, the popular jazz artist, gave us the new metaphor for teachers working together in schools. Some of us at Denali liked jazz. We'd listen to Wynton Marsalis and other jazz artists in the school gym at the end of the day, and at special times we'd dance and "swing." After the "messin' 'round" that we'd do there, we'd sometimes ask ourselves, "What does good jazz music have to do with our lives here?" Over the years, a kind of composite answer evolved that goes something like this explanation from the one of the teachers, Carol, who really liked to move. "Swinging is a lot like life. You never know what's really going on in the lives of others round about. So you just enter in. You just unleash the power that is yourself. You let your soul come out. You listen carefully on the spot to what each other has to give. And you find the groove."

Developing an Attitude of Extraordinary Respect

As educators, we'd come to an understanding about how we were to be with one another in our school community. We realized that in any community, there were likely to be people we didn't particularly like, but like a family, we knew we had to live and deal with them. We knew there were people we didn't understand in our school community, but we also recognized that the way we thought things were with such people was probably not the way they were at all. We were constantly being surprised with the brilliance of each one of us. So we simply decided to go with it, to swing with it. In other words, we all relaxed, gave up our tight and hesitant ways, and we all began to *move*.

As we did that swing and learned to move together, we had some help from a story we read numerous times to one another from the book *The Different Drum* by M. Scott Peck (1987). The story, called "The Rabbi's Gift," is all about extraordinary respect. We found the story to be a good reminder about how we needed to be and move with one another at our school. This story helped us to become a learning community:

> There is a story, perhaps a myth. Typical of mythic stories, it has many versions. Also typical, the source of the version I am about to tell is obscure. I cannot remember whether I heard it or read it, or where or when. Furthermore, I do not even know the distortions I myself have made in it. All I know for certain is that this version came to me with a title. It is called "The Rabbi's Gift."
>
> The story concerns a monastery that had fallen upon hard times. Once a great order, as a result of waves of antimonastic persecution in the seventeenth and eighteenth centuries and the rise of secularism in the nineteenth, all its branch houses were lost and it had become decimated to the extent that there were only five monks left in the decaying mother house: the abbot and four others, all over seventy in age. Clearly it was a dying order.
>
> In the deep woods surrounding the monastery there was a little hut that a rabbi from a nearby town occasionally used for a hermitage. Through their many years of prayer and contemplation the old monks had become a bit psychic, so they could always sense when the rabbi was in his hermitage. "The rabbi is in the woods, the rabbi is in the woods again," they would whisper to each other. As he agonized over the imminent death of his order, it occurred to the abbot at one such time to visit the hermitage and ask the rabbi if by some possible chance he could offer any advice that might save the monastery.
>
> The rabbi welcomed the abbot at his hut. But when the abbot explained the purpose of his visit, the rabbi could only commiserate with him. "I know how it is," he exclaimed. "The spirit has gone out of the people. It is the same in my town. Almost no one comes to the synagogue anymore." So the old abbot and the old rabbi wept together. Then they read parts of the Torah and quietly spoke of deep things. The time came when the abbot had to leave. They embraced each other. "It has been a wonderful thing that we should

meet after all these years," the abbot said, "but I have still failed in my purpose for coming here. Is there nothing you can tell me, no piece of advice you can give me that would help me save my dying order?"

"No, I am sorry," the rabbi responded. "I have no advice to give. The only thing I can tell you is that the Messiah is one of you."

When the abbot returned to the monastery his fellow monks gathered around him to ask, "Well, what did the rabbi say?"

"He couldn't help," the abbot answered. 'We just wept and read the Torah together. The only thing he did say, just as I was leaving—it was something cryptic—was that the Messiah is one of us. I don't know what he meant."

In the days and weeks and months that followed, the old monks pondered this and wondered whether there was any possible significance to the rabbi's words. The Messiah is one of us? Could he possibly have meant one of us monks here at the monastery? If that's the case, which one? Do you suppose he meant the abbot? Yes, if he meant anyone, he probably meant Father Abbot. He has been our leader for more than a generation. On the other hand, he might have meant Brother Thomas. Certainly Brother Thomas is a holy man. Everyone knows that Thomas is a man of light. Certainly he could not have meant Brother Elred! Elred gets crotchety at times. But come to think of it, even though he is a thorn in people's sides, when you look back on it, Elred is virtually always right. Often very right. Maybe the rabbi did mean Brother Elred. But surely not Brother Phillip. Phillip is so passive, a real nobody. But then, almost mysteriously, he has a gift for somehow always being there when you need him. He just magically appears by your side. Maybe Phillip is the Messiah. Of course the rabbi didn't mean me. He couldn't possibly have meant me. I'm just an ordinary person. Yet supposing he did? Suppose I am the Messiah? O God, not me. I couldn't be that much for You, could I?

As they contemplated in this manner, the old monks began to treat each other with extraordinary respect on the off chance that one among them might be the Messiah. And on the off, off chance that each monk himself might be the Messiah, they began to treat themselves with extraordinary respect.

Because the forest in which it was situated was beautiful, it so happened that people still occasionally came to visit the monastery to picnic on its tiny lawn, to wander along some of its paths, even now and then to go into the dilapidated chapel to meditate. As they did so, without even being conscious of it, they sensed this aura of extraordinary respect that now began to surround the five old monks and seemed to radiate out from them and permeate the atmosphere of the place. There was something strangely attractive, even compelling, about it. Hardly knowing why, they began to come back to the monastery more frequently to picnic, to play, to pray. They began to bring their friends to show them this special place. And their friends brought their friends.

Then it happened that some of the younger men who came to visit the monastery started to talk more and more with the old monks. After a while one asked if he could join them. Then another. And another. So within a few years the monastery had once again become a thriving order and, thanks to the rabbi's gift, a vibrant center of light and spirituality in the realm. [Peck, 1987, pp. 13–15]

Chapter Four

Finding Out What They're Passionate About

Around the winter holidays, the superintendent called me in to suggest that I continue as the acting principal at Denali Elementary until the end of the school year. Feeling that as a school community we were on a roll, I accepted with delight. At the same time, I carried on my evening teaching at the university. So, in the dark of the Alaska winter, working two jobs, I was often tired and depending on my habit of running every day to help energize me physically.

Ken's Revelation

In midwinter, I ran regularly at the indoor track next to the university's ice skating rink. One day, as I was running around and around the periphery of the ice rink, a marvelous event began to unfold before my eyes. The hockey team was out of town, and there were only two figures on the ice, a father and a son. Ken, the dad, was teaching his son, Robert, to ice skate. Robert, developmentally disabled in a number of ways, definitely provided a teaching challenge for Ken. As I ran around the track, I found myself intrigued by the way Ken was working with Robert. "He's so patient," I thought. "I'm really impressed," I whispered to myself.

At the end of our time in the ice arena, I said to Ken, "I've watched you working with Robert over this past hour, and I am quite impressed. You worked with him so intently. You were so patient. You seemed to know just what to do. What's your secret, Ken?"

Ken's response surprised me and also eventually gave me continued motivation for my work at Denali Elementary. Ken's response:

"To work effectively with Robert, I always find out what he's passionate about, and then I just pour it on."

Ken went on to say that Robert cared deeply about only a couple of things in his life, and ice skating was one of those things. "So," Ken shared, "I go all out to encourage him in this passion of his."

I left the arena that evening understanding much more about my work as a school principal. It seemed to me that this was the form of encouragement that all of us who worked at the school needed to put into practice day after day.

A Parent's Passion

When I attended our next Tuesday morning meeting, I told the folks about my experience at the ice rink. Upon hearing the story, Jenny, a fourth-grade teacher, said to me: "There's nothing new in what you're telling us, David. Maybe you haven't noticed, but that's how you work with us." I felt honestly amazed at her response, and I listened further. "Find out what they're passionate about, then pour it on. I just figured that's been your personal guideline about how to be with us. Why do you think we're here? You've found out what we each deeply care about, and then you've supported us and encouraged us. Each one of us. Think of how you worked with Lois. She's a perfect example. Lois, retell your experience to David. Seems like he needs to hear it again, as an illustration of how he is with us."

"Well," Lois (a parent who had been a part of our conversations since that first day in the hallway) began, "there I was, sitting in this meeting, and I got to thinking about a conversation I'd had with you, David, the day before. You were asking me about my life in Fairbanks and my life before Fairbanks. So we ended up talking about my work on a farm in Minnesota as I was growing up. How I loved it so. How I miss it still. And how, really in my heart, I'm genuinely a farm girl. This is who I am. I told this to you, David.

"Well, here we were in this meeting talking about inquiry method and connecting our kids to the place where we live, and all of a sudden I said to myself, 'What we need here is a community garden, and this is my chance to lead the way.' I sat in silence, thinking that I didn't need to be a frustrated Minnesota farmer anymore. I can be a real farmer right here, right here at Denali School.

"So then I said out loud to you all, 'We need a community garden here. Each class can have a section. Maybe some families can have a plot, too. And we can learn about plants and vegetables, and we can work together in ways that would give us a sense of place.'

"I remember how I told you all, 'If you think this makes sense, I'll set it up.' Remember how I said, 'I've got friends at Cooperative Extension who'll lend me stuff. So just give the word.'?

"Do you remember how you all said, 'Lois, go right ahead!'?"

Later that spring, on the first sunny spring day in May, there was Lois coming down Airport Way on the John Deere tractor she'd borrowed from Cooperative Extension at the university. As I looked out my office window, there was Lois plowing up the earth just outside of the school. "Oh, my gosh," I said to myself, "we haven't checked for underground utilities! You're always supposed to 'Call Before You Dig.' I just know we're going to turn off the lights all over town." Fortunately, Lois didn't hit any wires or culverts. She just churned the earth, and in the process started something churning that became just grand. She'd initiated our Discovery School garden. And she'd touched a spark within her that changed her life, while it also changed ours.

Lois went on to coordinate the creation of The Garden People, a group of about thirty parents, neighbors, teachers, and children who created a wonderful space for all the children, a space that encouraged the building of cold frames, greenhouses, and the love of gardening in the lives of the children. Our garden reflected the group's love of growing things and represented our school community's love of the growth process in our children and ourselves. We were a team working together toward everyone's growth. Within a couple of years, Denali children were consistent blue ribbon winners at the Alaska State Fair. All of this because one person was able to practice and teach what she truly cared about. Lois expressed her passion for gardening with the Denali community. And the children learned the love of growing things because Lois was, in her words, "at home" in her work. She was doing work that she loved for the benefit of the entire community.

A Teacher's Passion

The following year, Emily, a teacher, told a similar story. I remember it as going something like this: "As this Discovery School program began to develop, I noticed how everyone seemed to be getting aboard the bandwagon and how it seemed pretty exciting to lots of people, but you know, I just didn't feel much excitement about what was going on. Let's face it, I had my hands full with the difficult class I'd been given. Besides, I had my share of problems with my own kids with my husband being out of town a lot. So, believe me, I had very little interest in what was going on here. Zero interest, practically. Then there was that conversation I had with you, David, on that winter afternoon last year. Do you remember that talk?"

"I'll never forget that talk, Emily." I smiled as I told her, in front of the group, "It was, at the time, a difficult experience for me, too, but I think it led to a reward for both of us. I'll tell the story from my point of view, then you tell it from yours.

"As I remember it, things were going quite well with our Discovery School planning. Excitement hung in the air; folks were quite wrapped up in the process of the renewal of an old school. Parents were becoming involved in the work. The children were happier than they'd been in quite some time. Most teachers were involved. But, I was concerned about you, Emily, and so after school one day, I went to see you. I decided to confront you with this question: 'Emily, isn't there anything we're doing here that interests you? The new science program? The garden work? The new computer class? Isn't there anything we're doing that you'd like to become a part of, here at the school?'

"*Silence*. I heard total silence for a really long time. I was becoming really uncomfortable, but I decided to tough it out and wait for some kind of response. I waited for what seemed like an eternity. Then you told me, 'Well, I'm really quite interested in this sister school program we've started with the elementary school in Japan.' I felt instant relief and knew that we might find a home for you, too, Emily, in the Discovery School team. You carried on, 'Of course, I did some traveling when we came up here from the Lower 48 a few years ago, but I've not seen much of the world, and I'd really like to travel more. I think that if I were to become involved in anything, it would be the sister school program.'

"Bingo! Here was something that Emily cared about. Immediately, I said to you, 'Well, you know, Emily, we need a coordinator for that program. The job pays $3,000. You'd coordinate all of the planning for the group of teachers, parents, and children who are going to Japan this summer. Then, you'd also get to do some traveling. I went last year, so I don't need to go again. What do you say? Would you like the job?' And you said, 'I think I'd like that a lot.'

"After I left Emily smiling, I got into my truck and dashed off to the Alaska USA Federal Credit Union, where I drew on my credit line account. I asked that a check for $3,000 be made out to Emily. And I gave you that check the next day. If the truth were known, there was no money available for the coordinator of the sister school program—either from the school or the school district. However, I just knew that I had to seize that moment when I clearly saw what you cared about. I needed to pour it on, since I now knew what you were passionate about.

"My $3,000 became worth, in my mind, three million dollars when I saw you deplane from that next summer's trip to Japan. Even after a nine-hour trip from Tokyo, you beamed with delight as you led the group off that plane at the Fairbanks airport. And, you know, Emily, in my opinion, your teaching has been spectacular in the year since the trip. Up until the time of that after-school conversation, I was worried that you would suffer from burnout. Now, in my opinion, you're one of our very best teachers. So, Emily, what's *your* side of the story? How was it for you? From your point of view, did I get this story right?"

"Well, David, you're pretty near right about me," replied Emily. "I did think about the Discovery School, 'This too shall pass.' But, you know, I got hooked. Your question got to me. I sat there thinking to myself, 'Aside from the Peace Corps–type dedication that I bring to the job, just what is it that I want to give to this job? Perhaps I've got an opportunity here to do something that I've always wanted to do with my life. Maybe this is my turn to be creative in some new ways.' So that's why I said what I did. And of course, that response really did change my life. Your question was a good one for me."

Some time later, I eventually received my $3,000 back in the form of accumulated small contributions from various community service groups such as the Kiwanis and Lions clubs and local businesses that wanted to support our sister school program in Japan. As well, the Denali Parent-Teacher Association added their financial assistance. When I was invited to speak to such groups about the progress at Denali Elementary, I told the story of finding an initially uninvolved but now eager volunteer to head up our sister school program. I also told of my spouse's dismay when she heard about my $3,000 withdrawal from our personal credit line. I asked these groups for their help. I said, "*Any* help that *any*one can give to help repay this loan in support of our sister school program will be greatly appreciated!"

Chapter Five

Simply Outrageous Might Be Just Perfect

Understanding the group's mission became our constant practice. Unlike some school staff groups that went off and figured out their mission statement once and for all, we were in a constant hubbub about what we were about. "No mission statement stuff for us," one teacher said. "We've got to be figuring it out day by day. Our vision is constantly evolving, and it makes no sense to nail it down."

As I think back on my time at Denali Elementary, the representative image that appears is of this group of people constantly and willingly on the move. While I was spending some of my time having one-on-one conversations with teachers, going door to door to meet the neighbors, and speaking with individual children, most of my time was spent amid a constant hubbub within little knots of people. These little knots were the constants of my life. Sometimes the little knots were joyous, sometimes sad, and sometimes rebellious, angry, and ready to slay dragons. One such time was when we fought Frank.

Ready to Go

Frank was a central office administrator. It appeared to us that he liked the direction in which our deliberations were taking us. "You folks are doing great work," Frank would say. "Keep it up." At school district meetings, Frank was always telling teachers and principals to figure out what they wanted at their schools, then "Go for it." "Be unique," he would say. "It would be good if one school became a school of the arts, another became a science school, and yet another focused on the languages." Because he gave the "Be unique" talk so often, many principals believed Frank's encouraging words about the desirability of diversity in school offerings and began working with their communities, identifying their distinctive qualities.

We were way ahead of the game in determining our uniqueness. "Unique is our middle name," we'd joke as we talked about "Frank's Invite" and went about the day-to-day business of creating a school unlike any we'd ever known before. Ours was a school with practices that grew out of the vision we'd discovered, and the practices had gotten us where we wanted to go. As it turned out, one of our practices brought the school into conflict with Frank, yet it let us know that we were a group on a mission and positively demonstrated the power of "leadership of the whole."

Once we had established our science and math program for the staff, it became necessary to release all the teachers so that they could attend what we called Friday School, to be held each Friday morning. (Although it is more common now across the country, in the early days of the Denali Project, the idea of releasing teachers for a partial day so that they could learn new content and methods was still somewhat unusual.) The teachers had also said that they'd be willing to come to school on Saturdays for some science and math instruction if they could go to school on Fridays as well. "That would be just an ideal way for us to get the science and math we lost out on earlier in our lives," the teachers said, "and we wouldn't be going to these stupid after-school-when-we're-so-tired in-services!"

So, with the help of a University of Alaska education professor, we wrote a proposal and received a grant from the State of Alaska for $50,000 so we could hire thirty permanent substitute teachers for the Friday School. Each Friday throughout the school year, professors from the university came to our library and taught the regular teachers. The State of Alaska grant made it possible for each teacher to have the same substitute each Friday. Our parents accepted the idea, the substitute pool loved the idea, and we thought Frank would approve our plan.

"A Ten-Day Advance Notice Is Required"

The Fairbanks School District had a policy for anticipated teacher absences. When a teacher knew of an upcoming professional meeting out of the district or on returning to school after a sick day, that teacher filled out a change-of-status form. It was no big deal. The secretaries were good about seeing to it that the forms were signed and routinely processed. So, as we prepared for our first Friday School, all our teachers completed the forms, and our secretary, Cindy, sent them on to Frank.

The next day, all the forms were returned; all were marked "Invalid, a ten-day advance notice is required. Call my office immediately.—Frank."

We were incensed. There had never been a policy that the change-of-status forms had to be completed ten days in advance. I called Frank and asked, "What's the deal?"

Frank replied, "Oh, the change-of-status forms; I just decided a ten-day rule would be good. Also, I don't think it's a good idea for all the teachers to be away from the children every Friday for a whole year."

I was flabbergasted. I said, "Frank, you knew all about our plans. This was no surprise. We've been counting on your support, and now with our first Friday School coming up later this week, we're really in a bind. Five UAF professors have made their plans for the day; we've got commitments from all the subs; and the teachers are all fired up. What are we to do?" I asked.

As I remember it, Frank's response was something like, "I don't know, and I don't care. David, you just have to learn to live with some defeats in life. This Friday School idea was flawed from the start. I think that the entire idea is *simply outrageous*. Besides, we can't let something like this get going in the district. It would be bad precedent, you know."

I relayed Frank's message at our staff meeting in the school library that afternoon. Several teachers held up their fists; others cussed the central office with words I'd never heard from them before; and the group became a truly ornery, snotty little knot. The little knot waved and swayed, moved up and down, and eventually moved in rebellion out into the hallway, declaring, "Let's talk with Cindy about this dreadful state of affairs. She'll know what we should do."

Unfortunately, Cindy didn't have an answer for the knot, now squashed into a crowded office space of perhaps twelve-by-eighteen feet.

The Kill-'Em-with-Kindness Approach

That little knot just scrunched in there, boiling away, everyone talking at once. First there was this suggestion, then that suggestion. We seemed woefully at a loss for what to do. Then Carol shouted, "Hush up everyone, we've got to think: How can we make this work?" We all hushed, quietly hoping a good idea would come.

After a moment, Carol exclaimed, "I've got the solution. Let's beat Frank at his own game. Let's use the kill-'em-with-kindness approach. Let's just call him back. David, that's your job. Say, 'Oh, we didn't know about this ten-day requirement, but we can live with it.' Then we put new dates on the forms, now two weeks ahead, and we call all our subs. Cindy, that's your job. And we call the UAF faculty and just tell them about our situation. I'll make all those calls. What do you say, group? Isn't this our best course?"

You could almost hear the little knot begin to sing "Happy Days Are Here Again!"

Happy days were, indeed, here again for the Denali children, teachers, and parents. Two weeks later, we held Friday School without a hitch, having submitted our forms with ten days' advance notice. Never again were we questioned about our subs, as Cindy promptly and regularly turned in change-of-status forms each Friday to be effective two weeks hence.

The Friday School was, all at the same time, enriching, invigorating, and exhausting. In the process of gathering week after week, we became a learning community—a community that learned together like kids again and oriented itself toward our students' learning in science and math. Moreover, I knew that through our experience with Frank, our teachers had come together. Instead of giving up, leadership had emerged from the staff, and everyone jointly had fought (with kindness) for what they believed was important. We had birthed a robust, powerful, and effective community. It was so robust, powerful, and effective that no one was going to be able to stop us from becoming what we, this school, wanted to be. At the next Tuesday morning meeting, one of our parents spoke for us all, summing up "Frank's Fiasco": "What Frank did not understand was that, sometimes, what seems simply outrageous might be just perfect. Our Friday School teacher release plan is just perfect for us. He needed to see this—from our point of view. Maybe at some future time in his life, he'll be willing to view things from a perspective unlike that of his own. That kind of openness would have gone a long way with us. We're chock-full of energy and just brimming with the knowledge we've needed, so we can determine what's just right for us. Together, we've truly been able to determine what we want for this school. Frank says 'outrageous'; I say '*just perfect*.'"

Chapter Six

Who Are the People?
What Are They Calling Out For?

During my time at Denali Elementary, I conversed with Oregon poet William Stafford at summer writing workshops I attended in Sitka, Alaska. In the summer following my first year at Denali, he and I talked about my beginning experience at the school. After listening to my summary of the year's work, he said to me, "You know, I believe that you're involved in an effort that's all about what the world is trying to be. In your case, your community is trying to figure out what it is and what it wants. From what you say to me about your work, I think you're really onto something there at the school. My advice to you is only this: Just continue dwelling with your people."

Dwelling in the Organization, Honoring the People

"Just continue dwelling with your people." These words have held me in their spell ever since William Stafford first gave them to me. In fact, these words may have changed the way I look upon my work. "Dwelling with my people"—is this what a principal does?

William Stafford had gone on to tell me, "You need to honor your organization, and honor each person who dwells in the place that you call a school."

"Honor? What does this mean?" I asked myself. "What does honoring the people mean? What does honoring the organization mean?" William Stafford's thoughts reminded me of a conference speech I'd heard in which Joe Jaworski, founder of the American Leadership Forum and author of the compelling book *Synchronicity*, suggested, in essence, that the leader's work is to discover what the system, the organization, finds interesting. He'd noted that aside from such important detective work, we are simply to honor the people. That's all there is to it.

Honoring, as I came to think of it, means deeply listening to each person with the intent to learn something about and from them. It means listening to what each person feels. It means listening to what each person has to say *and* to what each person doesn't say but yearns to say. It means listening for what each person yearns to be. And it's the same with an organization. In my case, the organization was the school community. We were to honor what the organization wanted to become. Both William Stafford and Joe Jaworski taught me that school leaders listen to their organization, just as they listen to the individual members of their organization. "School organizations have souls just like people do," William Stafford said to me, "and our work, as leaders, is to connect with those deeper parts, those souls, of both people individually and of people in groups."

I had already begun to appreciate the power of these ideas in the results of my first question, "What do you want for your children?" This talk with William Stafford affirmed my ongoing queries to individuals and the school community. He confirmed that my continuing to let go of what I wanted as the school leader, of any vision I had initially carried into the work, would honor and benefit the people. Whereas my first question had perhaps been a useful intuitive move that I'd blundered into, these (and other) conversations with William Stafford helped me understand what I had done, why it was important, and why it was working to all of our benefit. Now I began to take these ideas even more seriously and to use this philosophy more consciously—for example, in exploring our school's relationship with the Alaska Native community. I'll tell you part of the story here and part of it later in Chapter Eight.

Appreciating Alaska Native Ways of Knowing

In those conversations, William Stafford also had asked me to talk about the people I worked with at our school. I responded with percentages describing our student population and characterizing our staff; our staff comprised primarily Caucasians as well as a number of people of color, including several Alaska Natives. "You have an especially rich resource in your Alaska Native population, don't you?" he replied. "What do you think they bring to your community? What are they calling for?" All I could reply with at that point was a vague thought I had about Alaska Native peoples' relationship to Mother Earth. Perhaps based on what I'd said earlier about our school's science-math focus or our desire to have our children be givers, not takers, and stewards of Mother Earth or my nebulous response to his question, he prodded, "What ways do Alaska Natives know about taking care of Mother Earth that would be appropriate for the Denali children to learn?" I knew that I needed to understand more.

When I returned to Fairbanks in the fall of my second year as principal, I turned to an Alaska Native education colleague at the University of Alaska to learn more about science from an Alaska Native perspective. I also spoke with the school district's coordinator for Alaska Native education.

In addition, I shared my summer conversations with William Stafford at our continuing Tuesday morning meetings. Here we were, establishing a science-math Discovery School and determining the ways that our children could be givers and caretakers. One of our parents put the question this way: "How can we change our ways of living so that our automatic response becomes 'we take care of ourselves, we take care of one another, and we take care of the earth that is our home?'" Yes, here we were, trying to figure out things that had already been understood—not by us, but by others who were close by and who, we soon learned, were ever so willing to help us understand the earth that is our home.

In the midst of a particularly lively conversation about how such an understanding might become our way of life, Marjorie, an Alaska Native teacher, reminded us "This is the way my people, the Alaska Native peoples, have always lived their lives. It seems to me that the way we and our children make this a more automatic response is by involving more Native peoples in the work of this school. I'm embarrassed that it's taken me this long to point out to us all that this school is surrounded by Athabascan people, and that Fairbanks is home to many, many other Alaska Native peoples. So, why not establish an Alaska Native elders program at Denali? Invite the elders into the school to teach the children and to teach the staff. There are interesting facts and practices that my people have available—especially about earth science. These are understandings that my people have held for thousands of years and that kids in the school would find fascinating. I suggest that we create an elders room in the school and invite elders to be in residence here. We'd truly learn how to become givers, not takers, as a result of inviting Alaska Native elders to be here among us."

And so the school invited Alaska Native elders to be among us. They came enthusiastically. An existing program—which served as a resource for visiting classes across the district and was housed at another elementary school—moved to Denali with the blessing of the Fairbanks Native Association. Children around the district continued to make field trips to learn from our Alaska Native elders, but the program also significantly expanded to serve Denali children and staff in connection with our Discovery School focus. The elders taught us how to read the weather and the stars. They taught us which berries to eat and which ones to avoid. They taught us all the things that many of us adults had never learned in school.

More important, what they taught us best and what helped our group the most was their understanding of leadership. So much of what they shared was surprising to many of us. As an example, we learned that it's better for us to discover what a person knows than to have that person tell us. We learned that it's better for us to sleep on a cantankerous situation than to try to figure it out on the spot. We learned that a hundred days of silence might be just what we need to discover the next step for our group. But the truly transforming message that the elders taught us was that we needed to know each other very well before anything meaningful could happen in the group. Once we truly knew each other, then the group could become the leader.

The Group Becomes the Leader

I puzzled over these words. In an effort to understand this elder wisdom, I, and we as a group, practiced "sleeping on it" and "silence." Eventually, the words began to ring true. Gradually, we began to notice that in our group work we were beginning to practice leadership of the whole. Fewer and fewer meetings used a facilitator. More and more, the person with the necessary knowledge or the understanding stepped in to lead for part of the time, then stepped back when the call was clearly for someone with another kind of knowledge or understanding, and the next person would step forward. Frankly, it was a bit mysterious, and we were somewhat uncomfortable in the leaderless group situation, but in time, we came to trust this way of being.

This leadership of the whole was exemplified in our brief but daily 8 A.M. gatherings, which in the second year of our Discovery School program had replaced weekly staff meetings and bulletins. Whereas we worked with curriculum matters at our ongoing Friday School, I had instituted these before-school meetings to take care of immediate need-to-know matters and sustain our sense of community. It wasn't an easy sell to the staff; I asked the support of key teachers, who helped convince others that my plan was worth a try. We gathered in the school library to hear whatever cares and concerns the group brought forward. Although I made some needed announcements and shared information about principals' and school board meetings, most of the discussion was led by teachers, who shared teaching resources (such as a children's book that fit our theme) and raised everyday management concerns (for example, "The third graders need to be in from morning recess by 10:10 A.M. so that the fourth graders can have their fifteen minutes on the playground."). I thought of these meetings as being like a teakettle releasing stream; instead of boiling water overflowing and scalding everyone at a weekly staff meeting, we could release issues when the boiling first began and deal with them by letting off a little steam, then coming up with a solution.

Of course, we also celebrated:

"It's Julie's birthday, and I brought in her favorite coffee and doughnuts."

"Just want you guys to know that I'm pregnant!"

It was great to give hot news while it was still warm.

The group became the leader. These 8 A.M. gatherings were leaderless. No one looked to me as the principal or any other one person to begin the meeting. As soon as two or three people gathered in the library, animated conversations began and as more people came through the door, they entered into the ongoing talk. It was more like a family gathering for breakfast, trickling in, than it was a formal meeting.

Thus, the old way of having one person in charge became distasteful to us as a way of working. While attending district meetings had already been a chore, most of us now hated going to them, with their one-person rather than shared leadership, their inflexible agendas instead of evolving processes, and their vote taking rather than consensus building. Our way of being together had been shaped by the elders' presence and their gifts.

"Imagine That You Are a Midwife"

What came to me then and what has grown stronger in me with each passing day is that I need to be like a detective when it comes to a school community. It seemed to me then, and I know it surely now, that the organization, the school, has a life of its own. Indeed, the organization is an organism. Denali Elementary School as an organization was calling out to us to figure out what it wanted to be. Does this sound a bit bizarre? It seemed that way to me, for days upon days, at the time. But over time, I've become convinced that

Denali School was calling out boldly and strongly and that I needed to listen to it.

One of my favorite books is John Heider's *The Tao of Leadership* (1986). This book particularly invigorated and encouraged me during my days at Denali School. Heider writes: "Imagine that you are a midwife; you are assisting at someone else's birth. Facilitate what is happening rather than what you think ought to be happening. If you must take the lead, lead so that the mother is helped, yet still free and in charge. When the baby is born, the mother will rightly say: We did it ourselves!" (p. 33).

I tacked this quote above my desk at school; it prompted me to keep listening for the yearnings of individuals and the school community. It helped me notice and stay aware of individual staff members' unique talents and abilities that were seeking expression. When I got a hunch about what someone wanted to do with their life and work, I tried to assist them in some small way with what it was that they were wanting. Maybe this sounds a bit strange and intrusive. But this is what began to happen to me. I truly began to think that my work as a principal was supposed to be like a midwife's.

As I watched and listened, I noticed that as each person determined what he or she had to offer the Discovery School endeavor, we were gradually becoming a community. We were becoming a group of individuals who deeply cared about one another. And we cared about what we were creating. We were determining, within the group, what we—each of us—and what we—all of us—wanted to create. We were becoming artisans skilled in our individual crafts, and we artisans were building a learning community, enjoying sharing our skills and knowledge with one another as we created it together. With fascination, I observed and participated in this organic process.

Yet mostly the midwife quote reminded me of my walk with William Stafford and the wisdom he had shared with me. A midwife works with the mother and the baby, honoring those individuals and the natural process taking place so that they might call the birth their own. William Stafford had urged me, as a leader, like the mid-wife, to listen carefully to the people rather than merely my own thinking, asking "Who are the people? And what are they calling out for?" William Stafford had declared, "David, honor the people; it's the leader's work."

Chapter Seven

The Talking Circle

As the Tuesday morning meetings continued, we (in general) and I (especially) were making progress in finding out what all the teachers, parents, and community people in our midst felt passionate about. Of course, as we progressed in understanding our unique gifts and talents and developing our Discovery School, we made mistakes from time to time. One such time was highlighted dramatically when staff members and I attended a workshop far away from the school. At the outset of this incident, I felt that we had lost our sense of community. More to the point, I felt that I had lost my touch. In fact, I was thinking, "Maybe what's happened so far at the school is about to implode." I was very worried.

During the summer following my first year at Denali Elementary, a group of us traveled over six hundred miles by air from the Alaskan interior to a college in the small town of Sitka in southeastern Alaska to participate in a mentor-teacher program sponsored by the State Education Network. Most schools sent their principal and a teacher or, perhaps, two. Twelve of us from Denali Elementary School went. Community service groups had contributed a portion of our airfare; teachers paid some of their way; and the sponsoring network offered some scholarship aid. We were thrilled to attend!

The longer I served as principal at Denali Elementary, the more convinced I became that if a school was to become a true community, the members of that community had to be together off the school property. So I found different ways for us to go to retreats together, make presentations together, and have fun together.

Those opportunities we took to work and play together away from our school really paid off in blossoming, joyous teachers who became increasingly accessible to Denali's children. Gathering the staff together outside of school was a great way to celebrate the numerous important projects we were carrying out with and for children. Little did I know that sometimes those celebrations would—at least at the outset—look a lot like explosions.

While in Sitka, a first-year teacher and I had what felt to me like a fierce confrontation. Furiously, and in front of the other ten of us on the sidewalk, where other workshop participants were also gathered, she criticized me because she felt that I had not been available to and supportive of her. All I could spout at that moment were my apologies and the question, "How should we solve this?" We all moved into the chapel space at the college, where we began to discuss what to do about "David's problem." From the beginning, that's how we described the situation—as "David's problem." We talked about numerous solutions, such as my spending much more time with first-year teachers, both individually and as a group; a buddy system to link new and experienced teachers; and numerous other possibilities. While the encounter initially felt to me like an explosion, the content of her concerns and the group's subsequent discussions fell right in line with the focus of the mentor-teacher workshop.

As it turned out, Joan, one of our Alaska Native teachers, suggested the best solution, in relation to our total community and in relation to "David's problem." Right there in the sunken circle of the chapel—a sunken circle such as might be found in a media center or a fortunate kindergarten classroom—she taught us to use the talking circle, an Alaska Native practice. Her teaching changed my life. Of greater importance, her gift of the talking circle to all of us was directly responsible for consolidating the Denali staff as a genuine community, an authentic community in which people listened with the intent of learning something new and cared deeply about one another's passions and pains, going beyond simply tolerating one another, when difficulties arose.

As Joan taught us, in a talking circle, all members of the community sit in a circle on the floor and quietly prepare for a time of sharing. Then the sharing begins, and one person at a time holds a sacred object, which for us at Denali School was an eagle feather. (I recall being told by our Alaska Native teachers that the staff could appropriately use the talking circle and an eagle feather, provided that the circle was initiated by and the eagle feather belonged to and was shared by an Alaska Native person.) When each person in the circle holds the sacred object in turn, that person holds the floor for speaking. There is to be no interruption. The person speaking must begin by telling of his or her lineage. Then the person must tell the truth of her or his concerns, joys, and wishes. This day, the first-year teacher recommended that we focus on our community and, holding the eagle feather, she began her turn by telling us all that because of my inattention and lack of support, she didn't feel at all a part of the community. My turn came much later, but between this opening statement and my own, other teachers commented:

"I had no idea."

"If I'd only known, I could have helped you."

"I could also share some ways to work with parents."

Within our talking circle, "David's problem" quickly became "everyone's problem." Each one of us wanted to be noticed and attended to in caring ways. Joan shared her anxieties and difficulties about being new to the work, and so did I. As each person related worries, concerns, and urgent issues, we listened deeply and considered the ways that we might assist one another. Often we became very quiet, reflecting on each person, each concern. We determined what was to be done as a next step in regard to our school community. As a result of our talking about "David's problem," I spent much more time with first-year teachers, visiting their classrooms and talking informally in the hallways. Although we did not set up a formal mentoring program, teachers (especially those with more experience) took a much stronger interest in each other (especially the beginning teachers).

We sat in the talking circle numerous times over the coming years; always the focus was on our community. In fact, during the first fall months after our summer experience in Sitka, the talking circle operated as the preferred form for staff meetings. The talking circle also continued to be an important way for me to learn about each staff member's deep cares, concerns, and celebrations. The Sitka explosion had called me to task; although I thought I had been attending to each teacher's needs, that experience demanded that I ask myself whether I had truly been doing so. After Sitka, I took on the motto "Find out what they're passionate about, then pour it on" even more sincerely.

For us as a group, the talking circle now provided a sacred and hospitable space where we revealed and dealt with all sorts of passions, a respected and gracious space to dialogue about and reflect on those matters for which individuals and the group felt passion. We poured out our individual souls and in so doing, the group became the leader. Not only did we understand one another's passions but also our group felt more like a family (warts and all) than a collection of individuals in an organization.

As I remember my time at Denali Elementary, I miss the talking circle most. In fact, I ache, remembering Joan and the others. I am convinced that the talking circle made us one people. What was shared within the talking circle confirmed for me that we were truly onto something significant about the ways we were to be with one another. We were making connections between each individual's creative work and the entire group's feeling; each individual's work was providing all of us with a sense of purpose and a sense of place. Day by day, more and more of us were calling the Denali school community our home.

Chapter Eight

Walking Them Home

I didn't get it. Why didn't I ever see the Alaska Native parents in the school? The children were there. Sometimes they arrived at school a little late in the morning, but the Alaska Native children were always present at Denali School. They made up a significant presence, actually; almost 20 percent of the school were Alaska Native children.

But where were their parents? I just couldn't figure it out. Ever since becoming the principal of this Fairbanks, Alaska, elementary school, I'd searched for the Alaska Native parents. Generally, they didn't attend the back-to-school picnic. They usually didn't attend PTA meetings. Seldom did I see them before or after school, picking up their children. On only a rare occasion were they to be seen in the hallways. I just couldn't figure it out.

So one September morning, I asked one of our Alaska Native teachers to give me some clue that would help me solve the mystery. Before school one morning, in conversation with Marjorie, I shared: "There's something that's quite puzzling to me about this school. I'm wondering why we have Alaska Native parents so rarely in or around the school. I just can't figure it out, Marjorie. The children seem to like being here, and most of them are doing quite well. But where are their parents? Why don't we ever see the parents of these kids?"

Marjorie looked at me for a very long while before she answered, "These parents, most of them, had just awful experiences in school when they were children. They probably were in village schools where they were considered to be difficult students by the mostly white and nonnative teachers. Most likely they spoke their native language and found it hard to follow what those teachers demanded of them. In some situations, the children knew little English but were required to speak only English while in school. They were often punished if they spoke their native language. Especially in the church-sponsored schools, one of the purposes of schooling was to completely eliminate the native languages, replacing them with crystal-clear English. Under these conditions, the children who are now Denali parents must have been unhappy. Their parents were angry. In many village Alaska schools, it was just awful."

During just those few moments, talking with Marjorie in her second-grade classroom, the situation became clear but not the solution. I could see why no Alaska Native parent would ever want to come across the threshold of a school, including Denali School, after what they or their families had experienced. For sure, I could understand why they'd never want to go through that pain again. But I still didn't know what to do to solve the problem. "I really want an Alaska Native parent presence in this school," I told Marjorie. I truly wanted the parents in the classrooms, in the hallways, and actively engaged in the life of the school. "So what can we do, Marjorie?"

Moving a couple of steps closer to me, she said, "David, you're just going to have to walk them home." Marjorie suggested that I walk out six blocks from school the next morning and return, reporting to her what I noticed out there while the children were making their way to school. When I got back to Marjorie the next day, I told her that I had seen a group of Alaska Native parents coming to within six blocks of the school—just the distance she'd sent me out. The parents said good-bye to their children while pointing them in the direction of the school, then turned around, heading back to their homes. "Exactly," was Marjorie's response. "Six blocks is just about their safety limit. They'll come to that point but go no further. You're going to have to go out there and gradually coax them into the school. I know this seems a strange and unusual task for a principal, but if you want the parents here, you're going to have to demonstrate your welcoming spirit. Just saying that they will be welcome in the school won't do it. You're going to have to go out and gradually bring them in. It'll be slow going. Perhaps you'll make a half a block a week, but day after day, you can walk them into the school. My guess is that it'll take you twelve weeks to get them here."

So the next day, I was out there, six blocks away, as children began to walk toward the school. I thought the families and guardians who gathered looked surprised to see me. I could feel the intimidation they felt. Actually, it was a very quiet first meeting. They voiced soft-spoken "hellos" and "good mornings." After that, perhaps most parents thought they'd seen the last of me. But the next morning, there I was again, vowing to inch them forward toward the school. Making a point of smiling, I introduced myself to them, "My name is David Hagstrom, and I'm the principal of Denali School. Would you tell me your first name, please?" I also asked them, "Could you remind me of your child's name?" I wrote all this down in a little notebook so that I'd know which children belonged with which adults. I learned five first names that second morning. That's all. There was no measurable movement.

Actually, there was no territorial change along the sidewalk until the beginning of the second week, when I encouraged the group to cross the intersection with me and walk perhaps a quarter of a block closer to the school. On that occasion, I learned where four families lived in that downtown Fairbanks neighborhood.

"This brown house is ours," Martha pointed out.

"Here's where Jessie lives," another mother noted.

"We live in that trailer you see down this alleyway," announced a previously very cautious mom.

"Now we're getting somewhere," I told myself. As I hiked my way back to the school, I softly whispered to myself, "Yes, yes."

Over the next three months, we moved closer and closer to the school. Actually, during the month of December, the experience became kind of a "walk and talk" engagement. During that final month of what I was describing as my "parent visits," we'd stroll together within sight of the teachers and children who peered out at us from behind the school's front door. It was as though those inside the school were cheering us on, giving us the courage to make it past those final few houses between the parents and the school. We'd see our "encouragers" out of the corners of our eyes, and we'd grin a little.

On December 14, twenty-eight parents and I walked through the front door of the school and were greeted softly by three teachers and a few children who brought us hot chocolate and warm cookies. The teachers included Marjorie, my mentor in this endeavor, and the several other teachers who had generously taken on my before-school playground duties so that I could visit with the Alaska Native families on the sidewalk. They showed our new parents around the school and thanked them for coming. As it turned out, this was the beginning of a very strong relationship with the Alaska Native community in Fairbanks.

As you've read, we went on to dedicate a section of the building for Alaska Native education and recruited Native elders to teach in our school. Over the next few years, Denali School became "home" for many Alaska Native people. As time passed, parent after parent shared feelings of gratitude:

"It feels so cozy here," said Ernest.

"I'm really happy in this school" was Clara's reaction.

John shared: "Finally, here's my school."

Oscar graciously echoed Marjorie's words: "Thanks so much for walking me home."

Chapter Nine

Karaoke Homecoming

Wanda had just belted out "Deep in the Heart of Texas," and before that, Thomas had them all wailing on "Don't Let Your Babies Grow Up to Be Cowboys." Now it was my turn. What should I sing that would turn heads or get them excited or bring them to tears? I decided to have some fun with "I Left My Heart in San Francisco." It was a good choice. As I crooned the tune, the parents and teachers rolled their eyes and laughed good-naturedly. We were together and life was good!

All of us, eight teachers and parents, were having the time of our lives at a karaoke bar in Japan. Our elementary school in Alaska had been matched with our sister school here on the island of Hokkaido. Each year, thirty of us—ten children, ten teachers, and ten parents—traveled to this northernmost Japanese island for arranged home stays and to spend time in our sister school. It was always an incredible experience; we were treated like kings and queens. Of course, we tried our best to reciprocate, offering similar kinds of extraordinary hospitality when our Japanese counterparts visited Alaska each year.

On this particular evening, the parents and teachers had a night on the town. The children were all tucked into bed, watched over by their host parents. We, the U.S. parents and teachers, were told to "go out there into the night and have some fun." I'm not all that certain how or why we ended up at this particular karaoke bar, but there we were, most certainly having fun. It was quite a special evening. As I looked around, these Denali men and women were truly enjoying one another's company. Of course, some folks were drinking Japanese beer, but for the most part, the group was into soft drinks, conversation, and encouraging the principal—me—to "sing some more sweet songs."

And I did sing them some more songs. During the course of the evening, I sang "I Want To Hold Your Hand," "Blue Eyes Crying in the Rain," "Will the Circle Be Unbroken?" "What the World Needs Now," "Only the Lonely," and "Somewhere Over the Rainbow." It's simply amazing how a karaoke sound system can strengthen and purify one's voice! And the cards with full lyrics on them sure come in handy.

Soon it was closing time. All of the Japanese patrons left promptly at eleven o'clock. But it was clear; none of us were ready to leave. I asked our proprietor if it was okay for us to stay on.

The proprietor replied, "Oh, please do; stay here as long as you'd like. I have two hours of work to do here, and the law allows me to stay open until two o'clock. So please stay on. It would be an honor if you'd stay in my place for a little bit longer. You've brought a kind of specialness to this place. Please, please stay on."

And stay on we did. However, pretty soon the calls for more songs were no more, and the group seemed to want to come together in some different way. "Hey, David, don't you think it's time for us to talk?" As Richard called out that question to me, a hush of anticipation came into the room.

Wanda asked, "Why can't we be this way back home?"

Before we knew it, we'd brought ourselves together in a most unusual kind of PTA meeting. I thought, "Here we are, thousands of miles from home, in the middle of the night, about to have a conversation about a way to be with one another once we arrive back home in Fairbanks."

Then Greg provided us with *the* topic of conversation, a topic that we were later to call "The Karaoke Homecoming Rules."

The Karaoke Homecoming Rules

Before long, we found ourselves sharing ways that parents and teachers could have significant interactions with one another, day after day, "in the real world of bringing up the babies," as one parent put it. This same parent went on to say, "Child rearing is so difficult these days; I just wish I had a teacher-partner to help me in the day-to-day, as I try to figure out the best way to be with my Amanda in her growing-up time. Going to school events and helping out with homework is one thing, but I need help with the really important stuff. Why can't we, parents and teachers, raise these children together?"

Then Tom made the suggestion that we stayed with for the better part of an hour and a half: "It seems clear to me that we're deep into a different level of sharing. We all know that we came here to Japan because we care about our kids. And of course, we were curious about life here. And absolutely, we wanted an adventure! But mainly, we parents came along on this trip because we cared deeply about the school and our kids. So here we are, having the most amazing conversations—about our children, with their teachers— at a truly meaningful level. I've wanted this kind of thing to happen, on a regular basis, back in Fairbanks."

"Let's work out the ways we can make this happen back in Alaska," I suggested. "Let's develop some understandings for working as a team once we've arrived back home at Denali School, understandings that will help us do the important stuff together as parents and teachers." Within moments, we were engaged in an intense conversation about teamwork, about why and how teams thrive and succeed.

"What will ensure the success of our parent-teacher partnering, in terms of really making a difference in the lives of our children?" was the question put to us by one of our teachers. In response, we created seven rules (actually, guidelines), which I scribbled on a napkin. The Site Council, a schoolwide governance body made up of elected parents, teachers, and other staff, adopted the Karaoke Homecoming Rules on our return. Here they are:

- *Get to know one another beyond the surface greeting.* When people gathered for a meeting, we usually greeted each other with something like, "Hi Mary, how's the family?" But we needed to know one another better in order to understand one another's cares and perspectives, as well as to delve into deeper questions about the purpose and the life of the school. We knew that back home, when we prepared to move into the big issues and debates, we'd take time out at the start. At each meeting, we went around the table or the room responding to a prompt such as "The greatest challenge my son or daughter (niece/nephew) experiences in school is . . . "

- *Be willing to declare what we each want to create.* We promised not be intimidated by state, national, or even central office pressures to "do this" or to "do that" for the children in our care. We promised to take the time to get to know each child and what would be right for that child. Once we'd had our own conversations about what we wanted for our children, we'd be willing to investigate the wishes of those who only knew us from afar.

- *Find at least one thing that we all value.* We wanted to make certain we stood on the common ground of at least one value. The value of (as we had previously put it) "giving, not taking," the value of caring for human and natural worlds, and the value of selflessness often supported us.

- *Talk about the reasons we're doing the work.* Initially, the reasons offered were oriented toward a given parent's individual child; later, the reasons were directed more toward the good of the overall school. "My child needs lots of encouragement" became "I want this school to affirm all the children." Declaring the reasons we were doing the work helped us broach the issue of motives.

- *Begin to talk about the process of change.* Once we had acknowledged our individual backgrounds and motives, along with our common values and purposes, we examined reasons why people don't change. We began to imagine reasons why a person might feel they had something important to lose. For instance, a teacher might have collected years of materials and effective teaching methods that provided her security. A family member might have succeeded in school under one system and felt that his child was just like him in regard to his needs.

- *Determine a change we're all willing to make.* We promised one another that when we found ourselves involved in a difficult planning process, we'd find at least one (albeit minor, if necessary) aspect to approve and take as our next step. We believed that we always needed to be moving forward, whether it was one centimeter or twenty-five feet. It was important to us to not get stuck in negative thinking, a typical educational scourge and a prevalent phenomenon in our district at that time.

• *Have a lot of fun simply being together!* Of course, we had created these rules in a karaoke bar in Japan, an experience that couldn't be replicated. But we had taken one more step in building a team. Perhaps Peter could bring his guitar and play a song at the end of a meeting!

Team building is probably the most critical skill for a school leader to master. Given the benefit of hindsight, I am convinced that what happened at our school resulted from the ever-widening circle of the school community team. The team started with just five persons in the dark hallway when the question "What do you want for your children, here at Denali School?" was asked. The team expanded as a result of the Tuesday morning meetings. The team increased in size and influence with the Karaoke Homecoming Rules.

Build the Team, Then Celebrate the Effort

Years ago, a friend and mentor at the University of Illinois, Lloyd McCleary (his real name) passed on to me some "secret of life" words that made sense at the time and have only grown in their importance with the passing years. Mac told me, on the eve of my receiving a doctorate: "The only thing that you need to have learned in your years of study here is captured in seven words: Build the team, then celebrate the effort." He went on to share, "That's the heart of school leadership."

I've remembered those words, and I've tried over time to master the skills that are involved in team building. Community building or team building involves, I've discovered, the most basic of human relations practices. I learned early that we all want to be encouraged, and we all willingly accept honest expressions of appreciation. I believe it was Mark Twain who once commented, "I can live for an entire year on one genuine compliment." I have witnessed a myriad of tough situations that have been softened (and made more solvable) because of the wisely used combination of appreciation and encouragement. Because I've observed so many successful outcomes resulting from someone skillfully using just plain "people smarts," I decided many years ago that when I'm with children, teachers, and parents, I'm not the principal; I'm their coach.

Oh, I don't mean that I'm a "rah, rah, bash 'em, beat 'em" kind of guy. Rather, I'm the "find out their unique and special skills and cheer them on" type. At Denali School, I held the goal of discovering the skills and talents of at least five new adults each day. I tried to uncover the interests of teachers, parents, and neighbors quietly and without a lot of fanfare.

When I saw someone I didn't know very well, I'd introduce myself and I'd ask, "If you and I weren't standing here talking, how would you like to be passing your time?" After the shock of that question passed, folks would tell me the most interesting things. They'd say things like "I'd be learning how to speak the languages of the Alaska Native peoples" or "I'd be reading stories to a kid" or "I'd be building a magnificent garden" or "I'd be working in stained glass."

It was fascinating to listen to what the people cared about and learn what they really enjoyed doing with their lives. I began to realize that the people were truly telling me about their creative selves. After listening to what each person was creating (or wanted to create), I did my best to encourage the development of that wish or yearning within the setting of our school. I wanted them to bring their dreams alive—here in our school! And I was not totally surprised to find that as the people found their heartfelt interests validated, appreciated, and encouraged, they quickly joined our Denali team. As Mac also told me, "Take a genuine interest in a person, and watch the grand adventure unfold!" I've carried these words with me for just about forty years.

As you've read, the Denali story is, essentially, a story about team or community building. In the years since its occurrence, I've thought more deeply about the meaning of the Denali story. It's to this matter of making sense of the Denali Project that I now turn.

Part Two

Making Sense of the Denali Story

So now you've read my story. At Denali Elementary, we thought of ourselves as a "Discovery School" and in fact, that name fit us well in multiple ways. As a school community we had found our vision, rather than taking on an outside set of purposes. We wanted our children to be explorers and discoverers (and givers, not takers). Parents and teachers discovered dormant interests and passions and figured out ways to contribute their gifts and talents to the school and its children. Teachers discovered their love for learning science and math, subjects in which they had little, if any, background. As principal, I discovered new understandings about leadership and building a community of leaders.

Often, as I think back on what happened in Fairbanks, I wonder, "How did those things came to pass? What was all that about?" When I tell the story to some school groups, folks say that Denali School must have been a special case. But Denali is a real school. The cast of characters I've introduced to you are real people, with all the challenges and concerns that exist at every school, everywhere. We had the local district, as well as state and national agencies, breathing down our necks about school improvement and test results. We had personnel problems and evaluation issues, just like everyone else.

Perhaps the story you've read could be seen as simply outrageous. However, the ways we did things inspired us and became, as one parent had said, "just perfect" for us. As we got to know our children, as we discovered our talents and gifts, as we found the vision for our school, the perfect plan evolved for us. We were inspired because we were doing what was right *for us*.

People inside Alaska, but outside the project, folks who knew Denali Elementary and Fairbanks—for example, colleagues at the state Department of Education (DOE)—expressed amazement at the school community's discoveries and its activities. A group of four Alaska DOE specialists gathered for lunch with me one day when I visited them in Juneau, a meeting where we discussed the Denali Project and its impact. They said, "What's happening at Denali is nothing less than phenomenal. Just look at how some common school issues are usually dealt with, then look at what happens at Denali." Although I don't recall their exact words, I do remember that we went on to identify seven common school issues and contrast their usual treatment with our evolving practice at Denali School. Here's a composite review of our conversation, based on notes I took at the time:

1. *Bringing about change.* The usual approach is top-down, mandated change, which results in change that is periodic, occasional, and cyclical. Nothing lasts very long, because there is no ownership. At Denali, it's grassroots change. It's change from the inside out. Everyone feels ownership; therefore, changes that are decided on are lasting.

2. *Leadership.* The usual approach is a cautious, supervisory, inspector type of leadership that is quite unimaginative. There is usually a lack of trust. Teachers feel that they need to ask permission for every little thing. At Denali, there's an expanded leadership team that provides a variety of viewpoints and a leader who enables others to develop and succeed. The leader gives away his power.

3. *Staff development*. The usual approach is that everyone deals with innovations in the same way, at the same time. The central office often calls all the shots. Often, as a result of the one-size-fits-all approach, not much happens. At Denali, teachers are learners, and they develop their own unique talents and strengths, so innovation happens in different ways, at different times, as it makes sense for each situation, and only where it is needed. All the routine ways of doing business are changed as needed; everyone feels alive and vitalized because they are learning and growing in ways that are important to them and to the school community.

4. *Purpose and mission*. The usual approach is that purpose and mission are unarticulated, unspecified, and unclear. Often there's a lot of talk, but not much happens. At Denali, the school has been reoriented around what members of the school community have identified as most important for their children. People began with their hopes and wishes for their children and then established a very concrete plan.

5. *Community involvement*. The usual approach is that the school's administration attempts to rally support for goals and objectives that it, alone, has determined. Parents attend open houses and other such events but often feel alienated and uninvolved. When they do get involved, it's surface-level involvement. At Denali, staff and families decided together that they wanted to rebuild and revitalize their school. Together they found their shared vision. It's been a total community effort.

6. *School partnerships*. The usual approach is that there are few, if any, partnerships; occasionally a business will adopt a school. At Denali, partnerships are essential, and there is a wide variety of partnerships: school-university, school-business, and regional and international school-to-school partnerships. These partnerships provided critical resources to do the work of the Denali Project. Perhaps even more importantly, they helped us situate our work in a broader context and kept our community from being isolated and insular.

7. *School resources*. The usual approach is based on a scarcity model. Resources are thought of as simply not available. There is

usually a lot of complaining. At Denali, the people claimed an abundance model, adopting the attitude that anything is possible. As a result, the Denali folks have lots of resources and an exciting atmosphere. There is constant assistance coming from everywhere.

I agree with these comparisons. What are my other perceptions of what went on at Denali School? In Part Two, I elaborate on how I interpret the Denali stories and relate them to the phenomena of community development, school change, and leadership. Here is how I make sense of what happened at Denali School.

Chapter Ten

Creating a Community for Learning and Leading

Over the years, I've tried to "help people find a sense of community in the workplace." Those exact words have set the tone for my résumé for about thirty years. As with much of my learning earlier in life, my experience at Denali Elementary in Fairbanks deepened my knowing of that which I'd thought I understood previously. What became even clearer to me as a result of my experience at Denali was this: in order to truly establish a community for learning and leading in the workplace, three ingredients must be strongly present: (1) a form of "extended family," (2) an ongoing process for collectively and honorably finding a vision, and (3) participation by everyone in learning something new together.

The Denali Family

Denali Elementary was a school primed to develop into a flourishing extended family, because it already carried a rich social history and because, at the same time, many persons there were homesick. What I mean by "homesick" is that many persons there wished that they were somewhere else. Many Alaska Native persons wished that they were in their home villages. Many military families wished that they were back in the Lower 48 (the continental United States). Many women who'd come to interior Alaska because their men liked to hunt and fish wished that they were in less of a wilderness situation. And even those persons who were basically pleased that they were in an end-of-the-line kind of place missed where they'd once lived. And, virtually everyone's family lived somewhere else (village Alaska or the Lower 48).

Such feelings of being far from home aren't new or local only to Fairbanks, Alaska. Amazing social transformations occurred in the twentieth century, including the loss of communities in which people knew each other well. Now we tend to live in organizations. However, these organizations don't satisfy our heartfelt needs for connection, and we merely go through the motions of working in them. Years ago, in another time and place, I wrote these words about a people far from home: "A sense of quiet urgency has penetrated the basic fabric of our society in much the same way a cold fog settles over and into the land. Its approach, while steady and relentless, goes unnoticed until the chill. Suddenly lost, we strain and search for familiar ways, only to discover nothing. As a people, we are lost and searching helplessly. There is only the knowing that we're far from home" (Hagstrom, 1981, p. 1).

So when I suggested at Denali School that we have get-togethers (including holiday gatherings) for the faculty and their families as well as regular midweek potlucks at the school for students' families, both staff and families supported the proposals enthusiastically. Folks seemed hungry for opportunities to get to know one another and were ready to become part of a kind of family unit that was larger than their individual households. Picnics, parties, and PTA-sponsored gatherings were well attended by everyone in the Denali school community.

As a result of the positive experiences we had as an extended family at Denali School, I've come to believe that everywhere we must replace the idea of the school as organization with the idea of the school as extended family or the school as community. "School as organization" tends to put structure first, whereas "school as family or community" puts relationships and meaning at the heart of its work. While all schools, everywhere, may not have children, teachers, and parents who yearn to be somewhere else, all schools, everywhere, have the need for their people to feel more "at home."

Yet the notion of working as an extended family at Denali School meant more than living within a comfortable and supportive social network. We also had to work productively with all manner of persons, warts and all. Most families inevitably operate in dysfunctional ways from time to time, and at Denali, we occasionally experienced difficulties, such as at times when one teacher might inappropriately take out her anger on another. But as extended family, we knew we were in it together and there was no escaping. We had to be prepared to live and work with each other for better or worse. So we went out and had produced hundreds of bumper stickers that proudly proclaimed, "We Are the Denali Family!"

We worked as extended family as we went about finding our vision, discovering one another's passions, and incorporating them into our day-to-day activities as a group. We gradually learned that making the journey of becoming a good school as an extended family—along with finding our individual roles in and contributions to it—provided us with a sense of home. It is in the finding of home—finding feelings of being recognized, accepted, and appreciated—that people feel comfortable enough to express and exercise their leadership abilities. As a principal, I also began to think of this journey with my extended family at Denali as my home.

Working as an extended family was Denali School's response to societal changes and feelings of disconnection, alienation, and isolation, as well as feeling homesick in interior Alaska. However, these conditions put us in danger of easy "ain't it awful" talk. It would have been so easy to say "ain't it awful," and I certainly felt this way before stumbling into that first key question in the hallway. For some people, it's just how bad things are for them. However, as a result of my Denali experience, I am much more hopeful and interested in creating exciting new forms of family and village. I invite you, too, to make a shift in the way you think about the societal changes that are all around us. We can respond to the changes in ways other than "ain't it awful." We can take the hopeful stance, knowing that we can create organizations that are more like extended family or community.

Collectively and Honorably Finding a Vision

Often, principals are urged to have a vision of their own to take to and implement in a school. What we experienced at Denali School relative to having a vision sits closer to, yet also moves beyond, Peter Senge's notion that *all* the individuals in an organization need to create their personal visions before the organization can create its vision. At Denali, a climate of honoring each other was being developed; in this environment we genuinely tried to listen to one another with the intent of learning something new. Feeling recognized and respected, school community members talked openly, connecting their comments to others' remarks. Because staff and family members felt valued, they willingly offered their ideas about their own interests and passions alongside their ideas about how the overall school could be better for its children. They talked about what they wanted to create in their own lives, and as they did, they joined their interests and passions with the simultaneously emerging and evolving vision of the school and its community. We blended our personal interests and passions with what we believed was best for our children.

I think of the process of naming and shaping an image of what the school wants to become in the way we did at Denali as "finding a vision." The process of finding a vision draws out who people are and what they're calling for. The vision that's found might surprise the principal and the staff and the parents, as it did in the Denali school community's case. The vision that emerges depends on the nature of the student population and its needs; the makeup of the neighborhood; and the values, interests, and gifts of the school staff, the school's families, and the larger community.

At the time, we at Denali didn't know we were looking for a vision. We were just talking about what each of us wanted for our children. In so doing, we spoke about our own educational experiences, what we knew about our children, what teachers had learned in their licensure programs that they'd always wanted to try, and so on. The conversation was wide-ranging, concretely personal, and philosophical, too. At each Tuesday morning meeting, we'd patiently and purposefully ask the same question: "What do you want for your children, here at Denali School?" Interestingly, as new participants joined the group, those folks who had originated the conversation or who had spoken at earlier meetings often kept silent until newcomers had uttered their ideas. For months, we didn't write things down; no lists on chart paper waited for us to synthesize or codify them.

We didn't come at the conversation with the goal of finding a vision. There was no pressure to conclude the process by a certain date with a vision statement; indeed, I don't think we even used the word "vision"! We weren't tied to this particular purpose for our gatherings and conversations; we just wanted to explore what we wanted for our children.

In using the phrase "finding a vision," I don't mean to imply that one day on our conversational journey, we sighted a vision lying fully formed by the side of the road. Instead, we *were* actively seeking and searching as a group for an understanding of our children, their needs, and our hopes for them, all of which required negotiating individual understandings and desires. Over months of conversation, a relatively common understanding and plan of action evolved. In that sense, we'd found a vision that was right for us, rather than having one imposed.

As I've thought about the process of finding a vision over the intervening years, I've had to ask myself, "What if Denali or another school community I served found a vision that, in my heart, I deeply questioned? What if its found vision completely or fundamentally contradicted my values or did not, in my view, serve the children?" As a member of that school community, I would feel a right and an obligation to raise my questions and concerns in the course of the conversations and even again at the point where everyone began to feel a consensus. If the members of the school community weren't willing to stay involved in further conversation or felt convinced of their vision, I would perhaps have to consider leaving that principal's position because I wouldn't be the best person to energize and encourage their vision.

Participation by Everyone in
Learning Something New Together

Perhaps it appears obvious what the most important ingredient in creating a community climate for learning is: learning something! However, I'm talking about *everyone* learning something *new*, something they never knew before. Remember the point in the Denali story where we decided to become a science-math focus school, known as the Denali Discovery School, and we realized that we didn't have the content knowledge or the skills to deeply support our children's learning in those areas? We broke out into laughter at this point! In fact, we experienced some catharsis as we admitted our ignorance. We somehow expressed a willingness to let go of the teachers we had been and open up to the teachers we could become.

Fortunately, we didn't go the route that many projects do—retreating to safe ground—but plugged on to find a way to fill the gaps in our backgrounds, turning primarily to the University of Alaska for assistance. At Friday School, every one of us, I as principal included, learned about such things as global warming and its effects on layers of permafrost, calculating direction using the stars, hypothermia and winter wilderness survival techniques, along with associated mathematics concepts and skills in the areas of coordinate geometry, statistics, measurement, and probability. We learned computer skills at the same time. Really understanding and using such science phenomena, mathematics ideas, and computer skills was truly new.

Of course, it wasn't as simple as that; it's really difficult to admit that there's so much that you don't know. It took some doing for teachers to set aside in midcareer all those practices and methods learned so well during the years of teacher education classes, in-service workshops, and work in classrooms—to go from a steady stance of "I know how to do this" to the tentative wondering, "So how does this work?" Humility became our watchword, as we let go of what we knew and what had worked for us in the past. It was risk taking in an alarming form. All the familiar territory was slipping away fast. Perhaps it was the fact that we took these risks as a group that allowed any one of us to do so. Nevertheless, it was just that letting go that allowed us to become the joyous learners—and eventually, the marvelously reborn teachers—who we became. We discovered that in the new territory of the unknown, we became like little kids again, learning things that none of us had ever known before. It was truly a time both of intense innocence and profound wisdom for all of us. Most of us look back on this period in our lives and say things like "We had the time of our lives" or "I never had so much fun" or "It was a blast" or "I never knew I had it in me." A remark by Peter Senge to a conference I attended captures our experience at Denali School: "People's natural impulse to learn is unleashed when they are engaged in an endeavor they consider worthy of their fullest commitment."

In the process of learning something new together, we changed what might be called the school's agreements of belonging, those norms that guide which attitudes and behaviors fit with the school's nature. We changed our organization from a place where we taught by telling to a place where we asked "What's to be learned today?" In other words, the teachers didn't just come to teach anymore; they came to be involved in learning—their students' learning and their own. The parents didn't just accompany their children to school; they came to be involved in learning—their child's and, in some cases, their own. We all belonged to this community so that we could learn. It had become a learning community.

My observations are supported by a dissertation study out of Harvard University (Pomeroy, 1993) that examined the beliefs and teaching practices of three Denali teachers across grades K–5, using classroom observations and interviews, with the Discovery School activities as context. Deborah Pomeroy found that these teachers' classroom practices were informed by their beliefs about the nature of science (science knowledge) and how to teach science. But more important, the beliefs that these teachers held about how children learn even more strongly influenced their classroom practices. Their focus on children rather than subject matter as the basis for their planning and practice may have served well the Denali Project and their own learning within the Discovery School activities. Pomeroy speculated that perhaps these elementary teachers, given their lack of science background, hadn't been "contaminated" by experiences in university-based science classes. In a way, their lack of background in the sciences allowed genuine engagement in learning for both teachers and their students, an engagement that contributed to Denali School becoming a learning community. In the context of the Discovery School learning community, teachers discovered the world of science with the guidance of university mentors, using an inquiry method that those teachers could also take into their classrooms.

Finding a Vision and Creating a Learning Community Flows from the Work

The finding of a vision and the creation of a learning community at Denali School during the life of this project occurred as a result of our engaging in an inquiry about our children and our hopes for them, followed by an investigation of inquiry learning and becoming explorers inside the school. Neither the vision nor the learning community happened because we set out to make them happen. As principal, I didn't bring a vision to implement at Denali. Nor did the principal or a small group of teachers set a goal to make sure that staff and parents became a learning community. Instead, the school community's vision for itself flowed from our dialogue about the question "What do you want for your children, here at Denali School?" Instead, our learning community flowed from active and committed learning that supported our vision. We took a big risk for the sake of the children we loved and what flowed from that was a learning community. The outcomes of the Denali Project remind me of a wise thought offered to me by a community development facilitator many years ago, whose name I've long since forgotten: "Some things can readily be constructed, brick by brick, stage by stage. Others more or less build themselves and envelop us."

Chapter Eleven

Servant Leadership

What I've shared so far, in the form of what came to be called "the Denali story," has focused on one very brief period of my life. Arguably, it may have been the most significant time of my life. However, much led up to my time at Denali School, and much has happened since. Recently, I've been about the work of determining the thread that's run through all of my life. My mother believes that my interest in becoming a community builder developed early in my life, and one of the stories that follows attempts to look into that notion. As the years go by, I believe more and more that my life interests and passions also have been shaped by particular experiences. I've made life choices because of what I've seen in the world and because of the people I've met. Looking back over the years, I see that persons, on hearing about my interests and passions, have encouraged me. When I was an undergraduate student, John Burma (my sociology professor and adviser) encouraged me to get into "people work." While I was a master's degree student at Harvard, John Gaus (a history professor) encouraged me to take an interest in the makeup of communities. At the University of Illinois, Lloyd McCleary (my adviser in the school leadership department) encouraged me to move into the principalship. In my initial activity as a principal, Frank Christiansen and Joe Hill (central office administrators in the Evanston, Illinois, school district) encouraged me to become more deeply involved with families and other community members. Because of letters I initially wrote to them, Roland Barth and Henri Nouwen became friends of mine. They both affirmed my alternative leadership inclinations, helping me identify and name my practices. William Stafford and I became friends as a result of his traveling to the Sitka (Alaska) Writers' Symposium where I was a participant over the years. He always encouraged me in my work, particularly with his questions. And I had many other encouragers.

I've spent time recently trying to determine what these persons who were important to me were encouraging. As best I can understand it, my friends were encouraging an interest I've long protected and tried to develop. Yes, I've always been drawn to opportunities to create community. When I sense a group is longing to be pulled together, I feel compelled to try to support the growth of a family feeling among them (for example, this was part of my work at Denali School).

But there's more to my interests and passions than just creating a "we are family" feeling. Even more significant to me is the concept of servant leadership, a touchstone that guides me as I go about the creation of a sense of community in a school. This concept is best known from the work of Robert Greenleaf (1977), but I found my best reminder of it in the words of Clark Brody, a state-level school administrator in Oregon, who said, "A school leader must have a servant's heart." Those words truly resonate within me. That's the kind of leadership needed in our schools.

I'm certain that the "I have the right answer" kind of leadership is wrong. I know that bullying is wrong. I know that mandates and directives work only partially. The way we—as principals and central office administrators—can create a community of leaders in our schools is by serving the teachers, parents, and children connected with our schools. We create a community of leaders in our schools by creating an atmosphere of discovery, of encouragement, and of support.

Collaborating with my constituents in school communities to *find* the vision that's right for them, helping them to *grow* as leaders within the organization, and encouraging them to *utilize their passions* on behalf of the children and families they serve is the way to create a leadership community. With my every breath and with my every resource, I am supporting and encouraging others. These are my interests and passions.

I believe that such an attitude of service, along with a set of congruent behaviors, is required to create a community of leaders in our schools. Because I believe this is so, the words "The leader must have a servant's heart" are the words I offer to aspiring school leaders in graduate classes, retreats, and workshops. Attitudes and practices associated with servant leadership are the way that community building occurs.

Let me tell you a little more about how the idea of servant leadership came into my life and how it plays out in my leadership practice. To do so, I'll tell you a story about my visit with Henri Nouwen and then explain a poster that I made that captures my understanding of school leadership with just a few words. In my home office, I have posted my understandings on a large sign:

> Leadership is Being a Servant of the People,
> Their Poet and the Keeper of Their Dreams,
> and the New Pioneer Who Finds the Way
> to Make Their Hearts Sing.

Lose Yourself in the Work of the Group

During the time I was at Denali School, I was drawn to the writings of Harvard theologian Henri Nouwen. I would often begin my day by leafing through one or another of his books. I was as much inspired by Henri's life decisions as by his theology. Henri had elected to leave his prestigious professorship at Harvard to go to Toronto to live and work in a L'Arche Community. There, spending his time with developmentally disabled adults, he hoped to be of greater service than he had felt he was at Harvard.

I was so smitten with Henri's example that I began corresponding with him about my own work at Denali School. I believed that somehow Henri was meant to be one of my teachers relative to that work. After a series of letters back and forth, and after I had left my work at Denali, I boldly invited myself to meet with Henri at his Toronto L'Arche residence. Graciously, he asked simply, "When would you be available to spend time with me?" The week I spent with him quickly and clearly informed me about what it means to be a leader.

During our conversations in Toronto, Henri explained why what had happened at Denali School had happened. He encouraged me to trust myself in my leadership practice. "Trust yourself, David," he advised. "Listen to the thousand other voices with respect, but then go forth into that territory that is your 'birthright gift'—your very own special ability to know how to be with people. Then move out to sea with that gift and the people." Henri was telling me to move confidently into the changing and unknown future of my work with people, drawing on what I did know—how to be with them. Perhaps Henri's greatest gift to me during that Toronto visit was his parting and paradoxical perspective on servant leadership: "Lose yourself in the work of the group, then find yourself again, energizing the group."

These words captured precisely what had occurred for me at Denali School. I had stumbled upon the right question to ask; I had listened for the answer. I had watched and participated as the people determined what that answer meant, and then I had found myself again, energizing the group.

Find Yourself Again, Energizing the Group

After meeting with Henri, I thought back to my days at Denali. I realized that the Discovery School project that evolved was not at all what I'd expected to be doing at the school, but I had been wonderfully energized. Indeed, the fear that I'd initially felt about being able to do the job had been dissipated by my inadvertently living the paradox of losing myself in the group's activities and at the same time finding myself as I tried to nourish their efforts. I reflected on my belief that we pass energy on to others in the form of encouragement and support. For so many years, I'd held the belief that encouragement, if it was ever-present, would erase the fear in our lives. At Denali, I had finally comprehended that through encouraging others, my own fear was also eradicated.

At Denali, I'd felt fiercely optimistic but also rather humble. I recalled Roland Barth's (1990) counsel that principals needed less to be heroes than they did to be hero makers. During my leadership at Denali, I tried to assist others in getting done what was important to *them*, rather than merely what *I* deemed important. As a principal, I tried not to foist my will on people; I tried to recognize what was already there in their hearts and minds.

A Leader Is the People's Representative and Advocate

In the purest sense, a representative speaks for and works on behalf of the concerns and desires of the people. A principal leading with a servant's heart voices both what teachers, families, and community members articulate and what they may be unable to name. Becoming a spokesperson for the Denali community meant not that I knew and communicated what was right for them but that I faithfully represented their purposes and goals. At the same time, as a servant leader, the principal represents those who may be marginalized in the school or society. For instance, I felt like an advocate for Matthew, a child in need of protection and direction by adults, a child vulnerable to being lost in a school system or a social agency. Matthew lacked parental support. For example, his teacher or I often had to take him home when his parent failed to pick him up after school, and once his teacher sat with him overnight at the hospital when the parent could not be located. Matthew experienced academic and discipline problems, yet he expressed high hopes for himself. It was as though I had been commissioned to represent and advocate for Matthew and for all others like him, those who may not have been able to fully articulate their anguish, pain, hopes, and dreams.

Leadership Requires a Poet's Touch

While I may not always be clever with words, I am drawn to the elegant observations of poets. Poets speak from their own soul and at the same time articulate the human soul. Many poets listen into or beyond everyday matters, to deeply understand meanings and connections that may not be readily apparent in the moment or on the surface. In offering their interpretations and words, poets provide an alternative time and space wherein readers can connect with feelings and ideas that, if attended to head-on, might be inaccessible or off-putting. Similarly, the leader's life as servant also requires a poet's touch in that principals must deeply understand the humanity of the people they work with—including their condition and their yearnings—then gather into words and embody in actions their hopes and dreams.

The poet's touch is also felt in a leader's ability to use stories to help the group move steadily from where it is to where it wants to be. At Denali, we often used stories like "The Rabbi's Gift" to help us all get out of our ruts, climb out of our stuck places, and move to the higher ground where we knew more fully what was right and good for us and our children. Stories carried us to the new viewpoints that gave us insights we came to value.

As a servant leader, the principal can also help the group craft its own stories. The principal elicits individual's stories—stories that answer the questions "What am I passionate about?" "What do I truly care about?" "What do I want to create for myself and my loved ones?"—and promotes connections within the school community around those stories. As a result of the constant sharing of stories by each person, discoveries can be made both about the entire group, building the group's sense of itself, and about the individuals it contains.

Finally, a leader with a servant's heart helps to summon forth the story of the group itself, retelling episodes of the group's history—its achievements, obstacles, and foibles—a story that, over time and through constant revision with everyone's input, helps the group negotiate and claim its identity.

Leadership Is Being a "New Pioneer"

It seems to me today, as I look back on my time at Denali School, that my experience introduced me to the role of leader as a new pioneer. The concept of a pioneer, someone who breaks new ground, is familiar to us all. But, perhaps the picture of a pioneer that most readily comes to mind is an image of the lone trailblazer or of a group of people who lead the way for others to follow. This is not exactly the kind of pioneer I'm envisioning. Certainly, I was constantly called upon to enter totally unknown territory, to make bold and what felt to me like courageous moves, and to clear the way. What distinguishes my vision of a "new pioneer" from this more traditional one is that when the new pioneer leads with a servant's heart, he or she leads along the path that the group itself has decided it wants to travel and does so as a member of the group, albeit a member with special responsibilities.

In this chapter, I've explored servant leadership as a practice of an individual principal. In the next chapter, I move into how the group itself becomes the leader.

Chapter Twelve

The Group Can Become the Leader

The way of the servant leader is the way of inquiry rather than the way of information. The way of information involves the leader in imparting knowledge (usually his or her own or from some source of expertise outside the school community). The way of inquiry evokes participants' understandings, values, and intents, as well as their gifts and talents. Taking the way of inquiry allows the group to become the leader in the school community.

Asking Questions

Making inquiries elicits participants' perspectives, backgrounds, and goals. Asking questions in a group setting helps to turn discussions from one-on-one conversations in which the principal may feel responsible for having an answer, to group-based dialogues in which the interaction among numerous people develops a new synthesis or solution. At Denali School, questions and inquiries for numerous purposes constituted an important venue for us to discover and investigate, for us to take the next steps in our work together, and, ultimately, for the group to become the leader.

For instance, the question I stumbled upon in the dark hallway that broke open a new kind and level of discussion that I hadn't imagined was "What do you want for your children, here at Denali School?" This open-ended question served the school community well over time. It not only began our dialogue but also served later as a touchstone for us to revisit in order to keep focused on our intents and purposes. Over the course of several years, we often exclaimed, "The Denali Project and the Discovery School started with just one question!"

Big questions that also served as touchstones came from sources outside the school community, too. Recall William Stafford's two questions: Who are the people? And what are they calling out for? In the case of my work at Denali School, I took these questions primarily as guidance for myself as the principal; they provided a focus as I watched and listened to the Denali community in the process of our Discovery School development.

Another sort of big question, although it was not quite so philosophical in nature, nevertheless played an important role in the Denali Project. This question served as a bridge between our statements of values and goals and the action plans we later carried out. The Denali community had come to an understanding that our school's purpose was to provide an environment in which children were explorers and discoverers, as well as givers, not takers. We had set the subject focus as science and mathematics and had even named our enterprise a Discovery School. Then we asked ourselves (implicitly, at this point), "How can we make this happen?" and began to talk about action plans. We ran right up against the fact that virtually all of us as teachers (and me, as the principal) had very little depth of content background in mathematics and the sciences. Now we needed to ask ourselves the question more explicitly: "How can we make this happen?" As a result, we thought of the University of Alaska Fairbanks's world-class science program and began to think about ways to draw upon its resources. Although it's a simple question, asking "How can we make this happen?" may well have facilitated our movement across what many groups or organizations experience as a chasm between idea and enactment.

Finally, questions specific to difficult situations also helped us to proactively crawl out of stuck places and keep moving, even devise new ways of behaving, instead of becoming mired in minutiae, anger, or hurt feelings. You might remember Carol's question when Frank announced that a ten-day advance notice was required in order to request substitute teachers for our Friday School. She asked the snarling little knot in the school office, "How can we make this work?" Then there was the time at the Sitka conference when the first-year teacher confronted me about her feelings of isolation and alienation, which she felt had resulted from my lack of support. In desperation, I said to the ten other Denali teachers assembled on the sidewalk with us, "How should we solve this?"

Looking back on the Denali story, I've realized the significance that truly open-ended, broadly framed, and honest questions, especially those spoken aloud, played in opening up issues and creating opportunities for problem solving, as well as keeping the process moving. While making inquiries seems to be an obvious, perhaps even humanly natural thing to do in schools, my experience at Denali tells me that being ever conscious of the power of questions and their timing to facilitate connection between potential change and the people involved gives school leaders a way into relationship and school renewal. When a whole group is asked a key question and participants listen to each other's comments with honor (that is, listen with the intent to learn something), that key question can midwife the birth of something new. And the group, taking on leadership, can say, "We did it ourselves."

Relating a Movement Model to Organizational Change

Questions keep things moving when it comes to facilitating school change and renewal. Of course, any school leader concerned with school change wants to make sure that the process doesn't get stuck. However, I'm thinking about something more than keeping the ball rolling when I refer to a movement model.

Parker Palmer, in *The Courage to Teach: Exploring the Inner Landscape of a Teacher's Life*, elaborates four stages that describe a change process and that emphasize the way people relate to their work and to each other:

1. Isolated individuals make an inward decision to live divided no more, finding the center of their lives outside of institutions.

2. These individuals begin to discover one another and form communities of congruence that offer mutual support and opportunities to develop a shared vision.

3. These communities start going public, learning to convert their private concerns into the public issues they are and receiving vital critiques in the process.

4. A system of alternative rewards emerges to sustain the movement's vision and to put pressure for change on the standard institutional reward system. [Palmer, 1998, p. 166]

Palmer first speaks of the "divided" condition in which people are living and their decision to step out of that condition. People in schools usually live with conditions of fragmentation and division: teachers work in "side-by-side caves"; many teachers keep parents at arm's length; teachers and principals at best keep separate and often do battle; district-level administrators often police mandated reforms rather than support innovations, maintaining a split between levels of bureaucracy rather than uniting with school-level endeavors. Families and communities are split off from the schools, too. Schools operate disconnected from families and the larger community. Although I don't know whether isolated individuals associated with Denali School had previously made solitary inward decisions to live "divided no more," I do know that in the course of the development of the Denali Project and its Discovery School, many parents, teachers, university professors, and other community members who perhaps had been disaffected in their work or in their relationship to the school came together and learned how to live an undivided life as a community. Indeed, our entrée into this community life started with the observation that the school's children were living divided lives; the children were explorers and discoverers outside of school but not inside its four walls.

One of the critical aspects of the unfolding Denali Project oc-curred when the first five persons involved (the two parents, two teachers, and me) decided that for the second Tuesday morning meeting we would "each one, ask one." That is, each of us in atten-dance would ask at least one more person—another parent, teacher, child, or community member—to gather with us on the coming Tuesday. Through the lens of Palmer's description of movements, we were gathering in "communities of congruence," which, as you've read, allowed us to develop an alternative shared vision.

An even more significant aspect of the endeavor maturing on Tuesday mornings concerned the moral dimensions and moral strength of our focus on developing children as givers, not takers. We had taken a stand for what we felt was good and right, what made a difference for others in the world. The fact that we had stepped onto moral ground gave the endeavor greater firmness and let people know that we were involved in something big. In addi-tion, the huge and devastating *Exxon Valdez* oil spill galvanized moral indignation when it destroyed wildlife and livelihoods. Our community was fueled by taking a moral stance, and people were attracted to our emerging work because of it.

Then we went public. Initially, the Tuesday morning meetings drew larger and larger groups. Later, we went before the district's school board to request designation as a focus school, but only after a critique by the superintendent and his cabinet. In fact, the super-intendent's critique strengthened our endeavor considerably by directing us to develop a seven-year plan. Moreover, we went before the board of trustees of the University of Alaska Fairbanks to de-scribe our relationship with the Geophysical Institute and several professors in a variety of science departments. We also took our story to local service clubs.

Palmer's fourth stage considers change in the institution's re-ward system. In most schools, the rewards for teachers usually cen-ter on the sense of satisfaction they derive from their own classroom work; some teachers also maintain the benefit of autonomy by remaining isolated. Over time at Denali School, I saw that teachers and parents felt rewarded by belonging to something larger than themselves, which brought even deeper meaning to their individual efforts. I also observed the invigoration of being an active learner, which indeed was its own reward.

In hindsight, I can see that the Denali Project represents a movement model of renewal rather than a more traditional process of organizational change and reform. Like the movement model, our process focused on people and relationships first, instead of the nature and structure of the organization. We also considered individuals' sense of ownership in the existing situation rather than the well-being of the organization.

Second, as occurs in a movement, we started with ourselves, particularly our children. We then considered the requirements of the curriculum. This isn't to say that we ignored district mandates, but I am saying that they weren't our starting place. The lives and learning of our school's children and the adults associated with them was our beginning. We focused on learning, not mandates.

Third, in a related point, we identified what we needed to learn from an insider perspective. Typically, in-service workshops for teachers are based on what someone outside the school thinks needs to be fixed or reformed, using knowledge brought in from an outside perspective. We frequently called upon the gifts and talents of persons among us to realize the goals of our project and our children's learning. When we did go outside our community of teachers and families for expertise, we did so based on what we had determined we needed but didn't possess ourselves.

Fourth, our project evolved as if it were an organism, growing from one stage of work to another based on an apparent next step rather than on a master plan. However, once we agreed upon our next step, we identified strategic activities and sequenced them for effective achievement of our goals.

Fifth, through our experience of being part of a movement in which the previous four elements were central, individuals took on increased leadership and the group itself became a leader, a phenomenon that is usually absent when the focus in placed on changing the organization.

In the Denali community, we found, as Palmer (1998) says, that "as we find our place in the movement, we will discover that there is no essential conflict between loving to teach and working to reform education" (p. 183). We also found in our movement experience at Denali that we loved to learn and to lead.

The Group Becomes the Leader

I've referred numerous times to the idea that in the Denali Project, the group became the leader. This phrase clearly depicts how a collection of individuals began to function as a group taking on leadership—a group that determined its own values, purposes, and direction—through a process of dialogue on Tuesday mornings. In addition, I've used this phrase, for example, in the context of sharing how we learned about Alaska Native ways of knowing and being, describing the leaderless 8 A.M. gatherings in the school library, and speaking and listening in the talking circle. Just now, I've described how adopting both an inquiry model and a movement model also fosters the group becoming the leader. Just what do I mean by this phrase, "the group becomes the leader," and what does it mean for the principal?

The phrase is all about community, a community in which people of different perspectives are pretty much on the same wavelength. Rather than just one person or one perspective—the principal's or some small group's, in which people outside the school are pushing for something they think is right—a wider group of parents, teachers, and community members with varying viewpoints came together in dialogue about a key question and, in the process, identified its values and found its vision. I'm reminded that when I first arrived at Denali School, teachers would come to ask my permission for many activities. While I appreciated knowing what was going on, I often felt perplexed that they felt they needed my permission for so many things. During the growth of the Denali Project, we all came to know what was permissible because we came to know our shared values, purposes, and direction.

Just as important, this phrase "the group becomes the leader" also refers to the fact that everyone associated with the school community has rights and obligations to share their perceptions and ideas of the organization as a whole. They are invited, even urged, to do so. Typically, the principal is seen as the one looking for and attending to the big picture. When the group becomes the leader, the group also seeks to understand and give attention to the big picture. In other words, teachers and family or community members don't have to limit themselves to the concerns of the narrow role they play or the programs they supervise. It's okay for everyone to suggest and discuss in a broad group context their ideas about what the organization would look like at its best. When everyone is doing this, the group becomes the leader.

When the group becomes the leader, what started out as a collection of individuals transforms, in the best of situations, into a collective that is an entity itself. What, then, is the place of the principal? Lest you get the impression that I think that the principal is not needed or that the principal adopts a laissez-faire leadership approach, let me be clear: the principal remains an active and central member of the school community. Instead of being the point person, taking charge and directing people and the school's mission, the principal is a part of the group, albeit a person with special responsibilities. Essentially, the principal gathers with the rest of the school community around the organism that is the developing school's mission, instead of being the first person leading a set of followers. In other words, the image that comes to mind is that of the principal sitting in a circle with parents and teachers and community members rather than heading up a line as the head of the school.

The special responsibilities and activities of a principal who is a part of the school community center on evoking, energizing, and encouraging the entire school community. The principal asks key questions and honors what every participant says, listening with the intent to learn something new, as if she or he is a detective. The principal draws out, affirms, and supports the expression of the interests, passions, gifts, and talents of staff, parents, and community members associated with the school. She or he assists in the development and coordination of resources to support the vision the group has found. She or he clears away the bureaucratic red tape. The principal is an active and visible co-learner with teachers and families. The principal reminds the school community of its values, intents, and purposes and the direction it has determined.

In the end, the defining characteristic of the Denali Project became leadership by the group, with each person playing a part that expressed unique gifts and passions. A key open-ended question created space for dialogue about our school's children and our school's purposes. The staff, parents, and community embraced a movement model of change. And as the principal, rather than serving as the sole and isolated visionary, I became part of a team that determined the school's direction.

Chapter Thirteen

On Returning

I believe it was Elie Wiesel who observed that a school couldn't ever succeed in keeping alive its original vision or the aims of its founders. This past summer, I traveled back to Fairbanks after eight years of absence from that town, returning with a sense of fear and trepidation. Was what I remembered from the Denali Project's Discovery School time, in reality, much ado about nothing? Was the excitement about creating a focus school and identifying individual gifts and talents nothing more than a dim memory in the minds of the people there? I've always thought of myself as an initiator, an innovator, and a pioneer. At the same time, I've always known that I'm rather poor at maintenance. If I'd stayed on at Denali School, would the spell have been broken—for them and for me? Had I been just a "supernova leader" who was looked on in amazement at the outset but now was recalled with disdain, having burnt out? Was the Denali family much better off without me?

My inner critic has visited me often over the years since I left Denali School and Alaska, and people who have listened to these Denali stories in oral form have also sometimes questioned me and them. Overall, educators who wonder about Denali's success believe that it must have a special school to begin with. That is, they believe it must have been a small school, that the teachers were handpicked, that the parents had time to focus on the school, that the staff and parents already saw the world in the same way. The issue of whether the Denali Project was a special case even came to me in a recent dream.

The Tom Sergiovanni and Roland Barth Dream

In my dream, I'm watching—from above—the goings-on of a small town that exemplifies everything I've written about in the pages that precede these words. All of the people were using their "birthright gifts" (talents and passions) and so were "singing their true song." The entire town was involved in learning new things, things they had never known before. And the town had a sense of community unlike any other town in the world. At that point in the dream, Tom Sergiovanni—a well-known writer on educational leadership—appeared at stage right and declared, "Okay, David, your Denali approach worked in this town. Now I want to see you make it work in *all* towns." All of a sudden, I'm sitting on a window ledge alongside a street in another town, and the place is completely dead—awaiting the introduction of my "simply outrageous" approach. With Tom looking on from stage right, I am quite worried and concerned, sitting there all alone on my windowsill. All of a sudden, a comforting presence—whom I've since determined was Roland Barth, author of *Improving Schools from Within*—sits down next to me and says, "David, of course your simply outrageous approach will work here. This approach will work anywhere." My apologies go out to both Tom and Roland; this was my dream.

Was Denali Special?

The sandman had spoken! When people wonder whether Denali Elementary School was a special case, they're essentially asking about the applicability of the Denali processes to other settings. They may also be saying, "My situation is so bad. You certainly didn't have the concerns we have at my school." So let's take the "special" concerns mentioned above one at a time.

Denali Elementary was not a small school. When I began as principal, the school housed about four hundred students, which increased over the next several years to about five hundred students.

The increase resulted when families in the neighborhood who had sent their children to other Fairbanks schools returned and other neighborhoods were added to the school attendance area. The staff comprised approximately thirty persons, about two-thirds of them teachers.

I worked with the existing staff, until a handful of teachers, attracted by what we began doing at Denali, requested transfers into our school after my first year. When I arrived at Denali, I found that I liked the staff immediately, but I didn't sense that I was in the company of a group of extraordinary risk takers.

Denali families represented a wide cross section of the overall Fairbanks community. It's also fair to say that most of the parents, many of them single parents, were working-class people with jobs (sometimes a couple) and commitments. At Denali, we did not put out a general call for volunteers. Parents initially volunteered because they discovered that the talents and gifts they possessed were needed at the school. They would have a chance to do something in connection with the school that they loved to do and that would also potentially benefit their own child.

The staff and families associated with Denali School were a diverse lot, coming from different racial and ethnic groups, varying cultural traditions, contrasting political perspectives, and different parts of the Lower 48.

Denali Elementary did not begin as a special school, but it did become one.

A Confirmation

All of these issues and questions crowded into my consciousness as I anticipated my trip back to Alaska. To my great surprise, I was greeted enthusiastically at the airport by a Denali teacher with "Welcome home, David!" Once I was back in Fairbanks, my worst fears were not confirmed. I discovered on my return that Denali folks regarded our work together with fond memories and a great appreciation for the pioneering efforts. I felt my presence received in a way that could best be described as warm and hospitable. I found that some of the teachers and methods we'd used had been redistributed to other area schools. I was surprised to discover that many of the teachers who had been mainstays of the instructional team were now at other schools, instigating science initiatives that looked very much like the program we had begun more than ten years ago. While I had worried that the work might not be carried on at Denali School, it never crossed my mind that the project would have proliferated to other schools by way of teachers who had been reassigned to other locations in the district.

During my visit in Fairbanks, I had lunch with two science professors from the University of Alaska Fairbanks, both of whom had worked with the Denali Project. When I expressed my concern about the Discovery School ideas not amounting to much over the years, they looked at one another and me in disbelief.

"That's the furthest thing from the truth," said Jim.

Alan offered this thought about the lasting value of the Denali Project: "Over the years, when teachers who were initially at the heart of the project moved to other schools, they spread the influence of what you all did at Denali into their new settings."

Finally, what remains the most poignant recollection of my "return to what had been" came in the way I was received by the current principal, who has now been at Denali much longer than I was. He greeted me with affection and (I believe) an understanding of the true importance of my work then (and his work now). "So, what's the working title of your book?" he queried.

"*Honor the People; It's the Leader's Work,*" I responded.

"Well, that gets to the heart of it for sure," he said. "Long after we're forgotten as school leaders, the people here will remember how they felt honored, valued, and respected. They may not be able to express exactly how they were treated, but they know that they were welcomed—even cherished—here. That welcoming, that honoring, is now the way of life at Denali."

So perhaps honoring is my legacy at Denali School. That the Discovery School practices live on is good. That the people feel "honored"—that's best. In fact, it doesn't get any better than that.

Part Three

Lessons Learned
Along the Way

The stories in Part Three situate the Denali story and the sense
I've made of it in the broader context of my professional and personal life. It seems that I've known something about community
building almost all my life. I learned lessons about creating a neighborhood community in my childhood. I learned about creating a
sense of school community during my first experience as a principal in Illinois. Working with other principals in Alaska and across
the nation, I learned how to create environments to support the
development, renewal, and well-being of school leaders. I've realized not only that school leaders need to facilitate the creation of a
community of leaders in their own school community but also that
school leaders themselves benefit from environments that nourish
and sustain their vitality, knowledge, and skills. Finally, experiences
I've had with the medical community and on my travels overseas
have helped me more deeply understand the development of leadership and communities in schools.

I must have brought beliefs and tendencies, as well as other
experiences that shaped me and honed my skills related to leadership and community development in schools, to my work at Denali

Elementary. I explore such matters in "The Thread You Follow" and "Blue Bicycle Summer." Since leaving Denali Elementary, I've explored the role that different learning settings developed specifically for school leaders play in their growth and nourishment ("Bush Is Our Location, Not Our League," "Preparing Principals in a Different Way," and "Finding Our Way Back Home"). Finally, personal events recounted in "What Is Expected of Us?" and "What Do You Do for Your Living?" have helped me better understand my time at Denali School, as well as my beliefs about and practices of leadership and school community development. These stories, too, may seem outrageous. However, I hope they'll inspire.

Chapter Fourteen

The Thread You Follow

One of my favorite poems from William Stafford (1998) is this one:

The Way It Is

There is a thread you follow. It goes among
things that change. But it doesn't change.
People wonder about what things you are pursuing.
You have to explain about the thread.
But it is hard for others to see.
While you hold it you can't get lost.
Tragedies happen; people get hurt
or die; and you suffer and get old.
Nothing you do can stop time's unfolding.
You don't ever let go of the thread.

These days, my favorite question to ask on making a new friend is "What has your life taught you about the work that you do?" As the person earnestly runs back across a lifetime trying to come up with a satisfactory reply, I always receive a request that goes something like this: "Well, how about you? What has your life taught you about the work that you do?" If there is adequate time to reply, I tell a story or two from my past, such as the ones you're reading here. They form the thread that's woven its way through my life.

I was born into a tumultuous time at the end of the Great Depression. I was a firstborn whose father was in the hospital along with my mother and me. His was a serious illness that, when combined with the "no jobs and no money" life of the early 1930s, spelled sparse times for the three of us up until it was time for me to go to school. But extended family was our way of life on the west side of Chicago. All of my relatives (on both sides of the family) came to Chicago from Sweden, and they all settled within a six-block radius. We took care of one another in the good times and the bad. "I Ain't Got a Barrel of Money" was our theme song, and I remember belting out that song at many, many family gatherings. Except for the money issue, life was really good to me. My dad encouraged me. My mother adored me. And all the people in the neighborhood kept telling me that I was one swell kid!

According to my mother, my work as a community builder began at age four. Because our Chicago neighborhood was more like a small town, an end-of-the-road collection of just a few buildings, I was allowed to go door to door, giving my greetings to family and friends. In return, I'd be given cookies and other goodies. (My mother says that eventually she had to put a "don't feed me" sign on my back.) For me, my immediate reward was, of course, an instant treat! But as my mom tells it, there was a larger benefit for the neighborhood. After dinnertime, the neighbors would gather under the light of one particular street lamp. They'd laugh about that "cute little boy out begging again." Then, they'd inquire as to one another's health and well-being.

"So how's it going for you, Fran?"

"Do you need help with your garden, Clarence?" "Please let us know what we can do to make it easier for you, Ed."

In my mother's words, "Somehow, David, without knowing it, you had that knack for bringing people together."

However, I'm not so certain that my desire to create a sense of community had its origin at age four. What I do know is that I've always been interested in people.

It's interesting to hear my mother tell that story about me; however, my earliest recollection of a desire to bring people together comes from being on board an elevated transit train rather than under lamplight. Riding downtown to Chicago's Loop at about age nine to visit my Aunt Betty, I'd look out on tenement housing and wonder if the people felt alienated and alone. I never saw young people gathered together, and I worried that they were blue and all alone. This concern would eventually be translated into my lifelong belief that alienation and isolation are the world's major problems.

Years passed. I attended college and graduate school and decided to become a teacher. I now realize that my decision to go into teaching had everything to do with my belief that as an educator, I could bring people together in community. I wanted to do my part to alleviate the alienated condition of the world and to respond to people's isolation. In the deal, some of my own needs for connection were undoubtedly also met. My desire to bring people together in community found an even better home in my work as a principal. I remember how I began that work as a community builder; it began astride a blue bike! You'll read that story next.

Apparently, bringing people together is a way of life I've been called to live. "Our deepest calling is to grow into our own authentic selfhood, whether or not it conforms to some image of who we ought to be. As we do so, we will not only find the joy that every human seeks—we will also find our path of authentic service in the world. True vocation joins self and service, as Frederick Buechner asserts when he defines vocation as 'the place where your deep gladness meets the world's deep need'" (Palmer, 2000, p. 16). These words of Parker Palmer's, coupled with William Stafford's invitation to remember the thread we follow, form a frame for the stories that are told in this book. Palmer's words might also explain why, for all of my life, I've thought of myself as a joyful servant whose work involves bringing people together. Perhaps that early childhood image of the group gathered under the lamplight did, in truth, accurately predict my future. My thread, a deep sense of community, has been woven into every step I've taken across all the years.

Chapter Fifteen

Blue Bicycle Summer

"Look, here he comes now; he's coming to our house. And he's on that blue bike. Do you think he'll stay for lunch?"

When asked that question by her brother, Natasha thought for a moment and then went into the kitchen to see what was on the shelves. "We've got some pork and beans. Do you think that would make a good lunch for the new principal?" Natasha called out to her brother.

"Anything will do. And let's give him a Coke," brother Tony said to his sister and to the collection of seven other neighborhood kids that had gathered on the porch of their home near the intersection of Lake and Dodge in Evanston, Illinois.

Creating a New Community School

The year was 1967. Natasha and Tony's school, Foster Elementary, had been closed the year before as a part of a citywide desegregation effort. A citizen's panel had determined that it was morally unjustifiable to maintain an all-black school in the heart of a community that claimed to be an accepting place for all people. So the completely segregated Foster site was transformed into a laboratory school. With connections to Northwestern University, the new Martin Luther King Lab School accepted applications from all across town. While local neighborhood children could apply for acceptance to King Lab, only a few would be accepted. By far the majority of children in the old Foster School neighborhood would be traveling to outlying schools like the formerly all-white Willard School in the somewhat conservative far northwest corner of Evanston.

Just prior to 1967, I'd been happily serving as dean of students at a local junior college. My career path seemed to be leading me in the direction of college personnel work. I fully expected that I'd simply look for dean of students positions at the larger colleges, perhaps at places like Northwestern or the University of Illinois. But then I got caught up in the civil rights movement in Evanston. It was the 1960s, and some of my friends had participated in civil rights efforts in the South. While I did not participate in events like the Selma march, I did spend a lot of my time engaged in marches closer to home. Local real estate practices seemed to discourage "open housing," so I marched to try to provide greater housing opportunities for minorities. I marched for many other causes, too. As I marched, I became known as a dedicated activist caught up in a cause.

So I suppose it was not too surprising that friends in the cause began encouraging me to apply for the principal's job at Willard School. "You'd be so very helpful," these friends would tell me. "Because you live in northwest Evanston and your house is one block from the school, you'd be a neighborhood insider whose very presence would say to the locals, 'You have nothing to fear. Willard will continue to be a good school.'" My friends believed that my experience with the civil rights issues of the day could also help me bring sensitivity and effectiveness to the work that needed to be done in bringing mostly poor black kids into an all-white, upper-middle-class neighborhood school.

I was persuaded by my friends. "Perhaps," I said to myself, "there's nothing wrong with setting my career on the sideline for a while. This Willard job will allow me to do something really important with my life!" What I didn't yet know about myself in that late winter thirty-five years ago was the depth of my calling to a life of bringing people together. Had I understood myself more fully when considering my shift in career plans, I could have imagined that the Willard School job was truly close to the heart of things for me. I'd always cared so much about matters related to inclusion, and I despised knowing that some folks experienced extreme alienation. My deep gladness, my passion came when I had the chance to make people feel at home. If only I'd known then what I know now, I would have rejoiced, knowing that my deep gladness was about to meet the world's deep need and that I would soon fall in love with my work at Willard School.

So there I was, out delivering teacher and room assignments to every kid in the five-hundred-student school on my bicycle in early August of 1967. Everyone appreciated my bicycle deliveries. Parents and children living close to the school thought it was such a novel way to provide new school year information. Many nearby neighbors greeted me with "Hello, Doctor Dave!" And over the six-week period that I was delivering, I was treated to seven breakfasts, twenty-five lunches, seventeen suppers, and what seemed like gallons of coffee and Coke. Even for me, a person used to taking risks and doing somewhat unusual things, that summer spent on my blue bicycle was an invigorating experience!

The notion of delivering the class assignments came as a result of the set of directions given to me by the outgoing principal. "When it comes to letting parents know about their child's teacher for the next year, here's how you do it," she told me. "Once you've determined the class assignments, get the information onto postcards addressed to parents. Wait until the Friday before Labor Day, and on that day—after the last pickup of the day—dump all of the postcards in the mailbox right in front of Carl's gas station. That way, the post office people will pick up the cards on Saturday morning, and they'll be delivered on the day after Labor Day. Because school starts on the Wednesday after Labor Day and there will be no one at school on Tuesday (since everyone will be attending the back-to-school meeting at the central office), there will be no opportunity for parents to fuss and fume about their child's assignment.

This method cuts way back on the grief factor for the principal. If you remember nothing else that I tell you, be sure to remember this, and you'll be off to a great start with your new work. Now, are sure that you're going to remember?"

Well, I remembered, and I was appalled! Especially this year, when lots of people would be new to the school, it would be just awful for parents to receive news about their child's classroom assignment in the way described by my predecessor. I began to wonder how I could best ensure that everyone felt included. And how could I have some fun while making sure that each family felt invited and welcomed? My blue bicycle summer resulted from that wondering. It turned out that my messenger tasks created gigantic amounts of goodwill.

Inspiring a Community

Natasha turned to me when I pulled up to her house. "Hello Mr. Principal. I just knew that you'd come to my house. My mama said you'd be too busy to come all this way. But I just knew that you'd come. I saw you comin' from a long way off. I've been waiting for you for so long. Our mama's not home, but we've got lunch ready. Mama said it would be just fine for us to give you lunch in case you came to our house. She cleaned up the house, just in case. Mr. Principal, my brother, Tony, and I want to know, do you like pork and beans?"

I share this story, not only because it is an example of a rather outrageous way of doing a principal's work but also because it turned out that this activity inspired community. It helped to begin building a sense of community within our school that, overnight, held a new mix of children and parents. Not only had a spirit of goodwill been created among our new constituents, but also this activity began to create a reservoir of talented potential leaders for the school. Parents new to our school community eagerly volunteered to work in the lunchroom, assist with neighborhood meetings, help with carpools when the bus broke down, and do anything they could to help create a new school community.

The story of my blue bicycle summer lived on for years at that school. While I'll never say that we were problem-free as a newly desegregated school, I can easily relate that right from the start we were a community that wanted to make desegregation work. I can't help but believe that the blue bicycle summer helped!

Chapter Sixteen

Bush Is Our Location,
Not Our League

Ned Johnson was a tall man with graying hair and a passion. For the most part, he loved the work he did as principal of a small village school outside of Bethel, Alaska. Ned spoke to me about the children and teachers with whom he worked: "These children have such stories to tell about their lives on the ice and in the snow. They know their world deeply and fully, and they are simply thrilled on sensing your slightest interest in the bush location that is their home. And the village teachers, they're top of the line. I think the teachers in the village schools are as good as any in the nation. What makes the teachers so good is their ability to meet the individual needs of the children and their knack for using this natural setting of rural Alaska to make their teaching come alive."

Despite his enthusiasm, Ned also expressed frustration, saying, "I feel so alone here in my work. There are different kinds of isolation, you know, starting with the geography. The village sits on the river, with transportation by boat in the summer and snow machine in the winter, but basically, the village sits by itself. As you know, we have only the one school and I'm the only principal, so if I wanted to talk to another principal face to face, I'd have to get on a plane. And then there's the racial distance and the cultural distance between my upbringing and the village culture. Those will always be factors, no matter how I learn to fit in." Ned carried on with this theme: "As a white guy, I'm a minority in this Alaska Native village, something I've experienced before here in Alaska, but it's still a challenge for me. Of course, the teachers at my school also sometimes feel isolated. They feel what I feel. We're the outsiders. We've entered this Alaska Native world from the outside, from Montana or Oklahoma or Washington state. It's intriguing to get a glimpse of another culture, and for the most part, I'm accepted by the village. My work is appreciated, and I go to most of the village meetings. I take steam with the elders; I go to the steam baths with them at the end of the day. It's good to be a part of this village. And yet I also feel so incredibly alone here."

Craving Connection

I was engaged in a research study sponsored by a state agency, attempting to identify high schools that offered quality education for their rural students and that had developed working connections between the school and village community. My colleagues and I visited a representative sample of bush high schools, so frequently I boarded small airplanes to spend several days in a village, sleeping on the gym floor in many schools across Alaska. It was fascinating to see the differences in the schools; some schools were making it, and others were not. Some teachers were simply putting in their time. Most of the educators, however, were highly attuned to the culture of their small communities and were extraordinarily skilled and ever so creative in their work. There were autumn writing campouts in which teachers lived with their students alongside a fast-moving stream, watching for animal life and using journals to record what they saw. There was a boat-building class in which the students were taught by elders in the village how to craft seaworthy vessels that could be used in the whale hunts so essential to their village's cultural survival. There was a class developed by a high school principal-teacher and his students in southeast Alaska, in which they prepared and packed salmon and then sold the fish to the Alaska Marine Highway fleet of ferryboats serving their communities. These students learned business skills, mathematics, and science related to the health of the seas and rivers, as well as ways to market their product. When we questioned this principal-teacher about his work, he said, "Oh yes, this is very exciting and quite meaningful work. There's a need here, and we're meeting the need head-on. I just love the work that I do. But there's just one problem: I don't have anyone I can really talk to about my being such an outsider to this community. I'd give anything to be able to talk face to face on a regular basis with a counterpart in the next village or down the line. You know, I can't just pop in a car and drive there. But here, I'm learning a new language and cultural ways that are new to me. Still, sometimes I just crave what I once knew and understood. Where is my true-blue friend at the end of the day? You know, David, sometimes I think I'll go stark raving mad here. I'm feeling so very all by myself."

It didn't take me very much time to catch on to this longing held by such principals and teachers, this desire to be connected, somehow and in a predictable way, to their colleagues and counterparts across Alaska. It was clear to me that the leaders I was visiting in the village schools were talented and creative but also starving for lack of contact with their own cultural roots—their culture of origin and the culture of educators. Understanding and appreciating their new cultural setting was good and important; however, these folks wanted and needed a lifeline to what they knew and where they felt they belonged. They wanted, at least occasionally, to associate with members of their own cultural family and to share stories about their new and different work with other educators. Of course, a critical concern, then as well as now, pertained to the compelling need for more Alaska Native school leaders and teachers. At the same time, the nonnative principals and teachers such as those I'd visited needed their experiences acknowledged and their spirits sustained if they were to continue to offer their best selves to the communities they served.

Making Connection

So Ned Johnson and I began to think about ways for rural school educators to have occasional get-togethers away from the villages. At the time, the idea of principals and principal-teachers coming together from all across Alaska was an outrageous one. "It takes away from what the state principals' association is trying to do," said one Anchorage principal, referring to the association's desire to have a fully statewide meeting, even though the rural principals often said they could not find sessions appropriate to their needs. "It will make the rural principals feel even more like outsiders in the association," a state association officer told me. Nevertheless, Ned thought that the best time for principals and principal-teachers from small, rural villages to gather would be just before the annual state principals' meeting in Anchorage. "Let's just come early or stay after the October meeting. That way, most of our expenses will be taken care of, and we won't have to make such a big deal about meeting on our own." For two years, we did meet in conjunction with the principals' association. But quickly it became apparent that school leaders in rural Alaska needed and wanted a very different kind of forum for the expression of their cares and concerns. As a result, in the mid-1980s, forty rural school educators met in Fairbanks and formed Alaska's Rural Schools Leadership Network.

The network sponsored an annual weeklong meeting in Fairbanks in mid-June. Principals spent time debriefing the preceding year's accomplishments, along with its trials and tribulations. Each participant had the opportunity, in a climate of complete confidentiality, to tell what went right and what went wrong during the just-completed school year. Participants would tell stories, show slides and videos, and express thoughts that were sometimes joyful and sometimes full of anxiety and fear. This debriefing process would continue until it was over, no matter how long it took. Sometimes it took only a day for folks to tell their stories, and sometimes the expressions of joy and hysteria went on for the better part of a week! After the debriefing session came presentations and discussions of new thoughts and approaches (for example, curriculum and instructional strategies or leadership practices, such as ways to involve Native elders in the school), usually from persons within the group whom Ned and I had invited before the meeting to share their ideas. Examining the topics that we discussed over the years, I find in my agenda notes the following titles: "How Can We as Principals Encourage a Greater Sense of Community in Our Schools?" "How to Build Shared Leadership for Our Village Schools," and "How Are We to Encourage Village Culture While Maintaining Our Own Sense of Identity?" Ned and I wanted to support principals in the development of concerted efforts to bring schools and their villages together around a shared vision. We'd end our week together by planning programs for the upcoming school year. Over the years, we discovered that once we had had opportunities to express our frustrations and had listened to new possibilities, we were invigorated to make new plans.

Over the years, Alaska's Rural Schools Leadership Network created multiple ways for its members to stay connected between June meetings. Eventually, teleconferencing arrangements enabled educators to stay in touch at least once a week. Every Tuesday evening, principals from across the state would gather for a conference call focused on a given topic. The most commonly repeated topic was how schools could develop positive working relationships with their communities. The network-sponsored journal recorded successful school practices from villages across Alaska. Network-sponsored teacher exchanges gained popularity. We still gathered before the October statewide principals' meeting. And the June meetings continued to bring together the disconnected.

A First-Class Motto

Ned Johnson's wish for connection and recognition was punctuated annually by the sign he'd hold up high for all to see:

Bush is our location, not our league

At the outset of the meeting, he'd wave this sign; at the close of our time together, he'd wave this sign. Despite the personal and professional challenges they experienced, these principals and principal-teachers felt proud to work in village schools located in the isolated, rural bush of Alaska. Ned's sign turned inside out the baseball expression "bush league" and made it into a statement of positive identity and belonging. Instead of being, at best, a second-rate, rag-tag group, Alaska's Rural Schools Leadership Network was to Ned and his colleagues a top-notch organization full of inventive and resourceful professionals. "Bush is our location, not our league" became their sustaining motto.

Over the years, members of Alaska's Rural Schools Leadership Network continued to talk about their joys and frustrations; they shared ways to improve their village schools; they considered how to build a community of leaders for those schools; and in the process, they also became a community of leaders themselves.

Chapter Seventeen

Preparing Principals in a Different Way

Picture this: A cohort of twenty-five diverse teachers, members of an alternative principal preparation program in Alaska, have gathered in the morning on a perfect summer day at the library of a high school for a meeting of the course "Building Community in Schools."

That day, we were focusing on the conditions that cultivate teachers' desires to become a team. To prime the pump, I asked the group, "At what times do you feel fully alive in your work as an educator?" In the sharing that followed, we explored the satisfactions of teaching that derive from individual classroom work. Then we turned to the rewards that come from community membership, the gratification that surfaces when a teacher contributes his or her individual gifts to the overall community endeavor and the way the community develops as a result.

Deep into this rolling conversation, Camille swept her arm across the air and called out to me, "Hey! Wait a minute! I feel totally joyful *right now* and when I feel totally joyful, I just have to sing!" Without waiting for my reply, Camille rose up from her chair and serenaded us all, filling the space with a robust rendition of "What the World Needs Now is Love, Sweet Love."

After Camille sang a couple more songs, another woman stood and offered us "Peace Is Flowing Like a River."

Then a third woman announced, "I'm going to a birthday party after class today, and I brought a guitar with me to play at the party. Let me get it." Until lunchtime, we all sang camp songs together to the accompaniment of her guitar. Although we didn't usually eat lunch together, everyone gathered spontaneously for a meal on the sunny deck of a local establishment.

There we had been, at the beginning of class, talking about the conditions that create a team, that foster the development of a community of leaders, and here we were, finishing our morning, saying, "We *did* it today!" Because Camille had freely and joyfully given us her gift of song, others had been encouraged to give their gifts, too. Something had gotten started, and in that process, community was being created. We had moved from connecting cerebrally, merely thinking about the idea of team building, to experiencing that very thing. Letting go into the spirit of what was happening, we connected and communicated on a different level, a heart level, allowing something larger than ourselves as a collection of individuals to emerge from us.

A Different Kind of Preparation for Principals

The story I've just recounted occurred in the context of a principal preparation program that I facilitated after my days at Denali Elementary. During my years at Denali, I realized that I wanted to share with would-be principals what we were learning there about becoming a community of leaders. Moreover, in the course of my many years working in principal licensure programs, I had come to question the preparation of our school leaders. I believe that new principals need to develop their relationship skills. I don't assume that just because a teacher has been successful in a classroom that they possess the capacities for communication with adults and capabilities to build community that are needed to be a leader serving an entire school community.

I also saw that principal preparation programs tend to emphasize matters of organizational management—for example, with courses in school finance and school law. They often lack a clear focus on relationship building and people skills, as well as program and curriculum development. While managing budgets and understanding laws affecting schools are both necessary, such areas take too much time away from a focus on learning, the purposes of schools, and working with people so as to foster those purposes. Furthermore, such programs are often taught by professors who haven't had much experience as principals.

I was also concerned that many participants in principal preparation programs enroll to secure a "just-in-case" credential, in case one day the right opportunity happens to roll around. The problems with principal preparation and some participants in those programs just didn't make sense to me.

Getting Started

I started talking with others around Alaska about offering an alternative to the preparation programs that were then available to potential school leaders. I spoke with the Alaska Association of School Administrators and members of the principals' organizations, professors at each of the three University of Alaska campuses, representatives of the State Department of Education, NEA Alaska (our statewide education association), individual school superintendents, and possible principal candidates. They all liked the idea. Many educators across Alaska wanted in as we created an alternative leadership preparation program, one which differed from traditional programs in its curriculum, teaching faculty, and students.

So a small representative group put the ideas together in the form of a white paper, which eventually led to a program proposal for the Alaska Center for Educational Leadership (AkCEL). Not knowing our chances, we sent our proposal to Washington, D.C., for consideration by the federal funders. Within a few months, we received word that we'd been awarded a very generous grant to "offer an alternative, experimental school leadership preparation program for the people of Alaska."

AkCEL's Unique Features

Almost immediately, we became operational. With representatives from the three branches of the University of Alaska, the statewide school administrator association, the Department of Education in Juneau and other interested parties, we outlined our program in a small brochure and got the word out to every part of Alaska.

AkCEL's Curriculum and Teaching Faculty

Our brochure described the design of the program and profiled our course offerings, which emphasized community-building and communication skills—that is, "people skills." Sure, we created an excellent school law course and found exceptionally talented experts to teach it. Sure, we paid attention to school finance issues, along with how to develop and manage a school budget. In our case, we stressed ways that the principal should involve the broad school community in shaping the budget. And of course, we included superb curriculum building and program development offerings. But what was extraordinary about the AkCEL program was our focus on meeting the needs of our diverse ethnic communities and on building a community of leaders in our schools.

To do so, we incorporated many of the attitudes, processes, and skills developed and used at Denali School that I believed every principal should possess and that weren't typically considered deeply (if at all) in most traditional preparation programs. Predominant among these beliefs, processes, and abilities were the following:

- Holding an uncompromising and unfailing belief in the people that constitute the school community
- Honoring the people by listening with the intent to learn something new about and from them
- Focusing on what the school community determines to be its needs and wants, then facilitating the development of the community's vision in a plan

- Identifying individual gifts, talents, and areas of passion, as well as inviting persons to offer them to support the school community's vision of its purposes
- Encouraging and energizing people and their work

We emphasized working with the wider school community, hearing from numerous panels of parents, community members, and children. We role-played different kinds of conversations that school leaders might have with families, teachers, and community groups, including a speech they would actually give to a Parent-Teacher Association meeting inviting their greater involvement in the future development of the school community. One assigned learning task required these would-be principals to interview five parents (from their own school) in the family's home, using the question, "What do you want for your child, here in this school?" They also interviewed legislators and businesspeople regarding their expectations for their school. Based on what they'd come to understand from these parents and other community members—and realizing that the small sample of people with whom they'd spoken represented only a portion of the school community—the prospective principals developed a proposal that tapped the passions and expertise of families and staff and also partnered with community resources surrounding the school. While this assignment has its limitations, including that such a proposal would, in real life, evolve more organically from the school community over time, it represented our best effort to simulate significant aspects of a principal's work in evoking, energizing, and encouraging a community of leaders.

The AkCEL teaching faculty, diverse in race, ethnicity, and gender, represented a balance of practitioners and university faculty from all three University of Alaska campuses. The practitioners ranged from principals, superintendents, and teachers to heads of organizations such as the Native Alaskan Science Project and the Alaska School Boards Association to corporate employees and businesspersons such as attorneys. Guest presenters, supported by the federal grant, traveled in from across the nation.

AkCEL Participants

Like other principal preparation programs, AkCEL required test scores, good grades, and letters of reference from its candidates. Here we diverged from then-routine admissions practices. We required that one of the references be from the applicant's superintendent or another member of the central office where the applicant was employed, indicating that he or she believed the applicant to be the type of person the writer thought should become a principal and that, if the person successfully completed the program, the district would seriously consider the newly prepared principal for openings. We personally interviewed each applicant, seeking to learn especially whether the applicant had committed themselves to school leadership and to remaining in Alaska. We tried to recruit and select applicants appropriate to diverse populations of students, including candidates of Alaska Native, African American, and other so-called minority backgrounds, women, and persons who found working in village schools attractive.

AkCEL Epilogue

Unfortunately, AkCEL is no more. Like so many other innovative projects, it didn't live beyond its soft money lifetime. I tried so hard during AkCEL's brief three-year existence to convince the University of Alaska to pick up the financial costs of the program and to replace existing offerings with the program that had, indeed, become the talk of school leaders around Alaska. But my hopes and my pleadings fell on deaf ears. The Alaska Center for Educational Leadership, as an alternative leadership preparation option, died at the end of the grant.

I felt as though a part of me had died as well. I felt disappointed, discouraged, and almost bereft. I felt that I had let down the participants by not ensuring the continuation of the program they had come to believe in. I felt that I had let down countless prospective leadership candidates who wanted just that kind of offering. And I felt that I had let down school districts that had come to count on AkCEL as a place to "grow their own principals." As the years have passed, I've felt better about our attempt. Some consolation has come from educators and others in Alaska, who tell me, "AkCEL was one of the most exciting and encouraging educational innovations in the history of the state" (words from a university professor in Alaska).

AkCEL-prepared principals have provided vibrant leadership for many Fairbanks schools, as well as other corners of Alaska. These principals tell me, "The day will come when the ideas we believed in will be front and center; we were just a little ahead of our time."

One AkCEL participant who has since moved to the southwestern United States e-mailed me, "The ideas are not dead; I've created a program with AkCEL-type qualities here."

Maybe all of the stories here are just a little ahead of their time. I'm rather hopeful that relationship building and community development are about to take center stage in the way we prepare principals.

Chapter Eighteen

Finding Our Way Back Home

"It's going to be close, David; there's a race going on inside of me, and the two participants are retirement or a heart attack. One or the other is going to win. There's no other way. Which will win? I'm only in my forties, and I hope I'll make it to retirement, but I'm worried that the job is going to get to me first. This work is simply killing me."

Paul's Story

These words from a high school educator greeted me on my arrival at his office late during the 1998-99 school year. I knew Paul as a teacher-leader enrolled in the school leadership program at Lewis & Clark College where I taught. While he wasn't oriented toward becoming a principal, Paul knew that if he wanted to obtain some kind of work in his district's central office, the state would require him to hold an administrative license.

Paul said he felt "caught between unrealistic demands of the administration, a totally irrational parent community, and the most militant colleagues on the face of the earth." He concluded, "I used to love to come to work; but now it seems like it is such a chore. I wish there were some other option. I need to find my way back to being the educator I once was. How can I find my way back to how I was? David, how can I find my way back home?"

I had no easy answers for my friend. He'd become my friend as a result of many heartfelt conversations at the end of school days over a whole year's time. Paul had enrolled in a graduate course I'd taught, and I decided to shadow him at work for one day. Following him around from dawn till dark left me exhausted but very impressed with his moral courage. Paul was a fellow who walked his talk and stepped way out front in making known his beliefs on topics from global justice issues to students' use of inappropriate language at lunchtimes. I saw in him the teacher he had decided to be almost twenty years before. As I followed Paul around that day, I said to myself, "This guy is terrific. Wouldn't it be wonderful if more educators were like Paul?"

Paul's Teacher Leadership

I'd been impressed with Paul from day one of our school leadership class. When he was invited to make some comments about his teaching and leadership career, Paul said that for years, he'd acted as what he called a "teacher-leader." As he explained it, "I never, not in a million years, thought of myself as being an administrator or principal type. I just loved teaching and, over the years, found myself sort of at the center of things in the school. What I did kind of made the school go round. I enjoyed being a mentor to the new teachers; I'd try my best to encourage them during their first couple of years. Of course, I just loved the kids. It's been kind of recent that I've considered myself a teacher-leader. I've been really happy as a teacher, now especially as I mentor new teachers. I've never wanted to be a principal. Why would anyone, I'd say to my wife, want to become a school principal? You'd just end up doing what no one else wanted to do. I even had days when I really hated the administration. But now I just might become one of them. On my good days as a teacher, I feel so creative and fully charged; I've had moments when I say to myself, 'This is just such good work.' But now, things are tough for me; I'll tell you more as the time goes on."

Paul first decided to become a high school teacher because he was so well regarded ("honored" was the word he used) by his own high school history teacher. "Mr. B. was interesting, inspiring, funny; he told the very best jokes, and he really invested himself in the kids. He really got me to thinking about what I wanted to do when I got out of school. By the time I was a junior, I was certain; I would be a teacher.

"The deal was clinched," Paul went on to say, "when I came back to see Mr. B. at semester break during my first year in college. When I told him that I would soon enter the teacher education program at Ohio State, he just glowed. He said to me, 'Paul, you're going to be a great teacher. I always thought you were cut out for this work. I think you're a lot like me. Chances are, you'll see this work as a calling, just as I have. For years, I've believed that teaching is my mission in life. I was called to this vocation,' Mr. B. told me. 'Me, too, Mr. B,' I said. 'This is how I want to spend my life.'"

As I leaned my back against Paul's office wall many years after what Paul refers to as his early, glory days in teaching, he told me of the decision he had made late the previous night to elect early retirement. He said to me, "David, I have no other choice. The joy has gone out of this job. My energy is spent, and I simply hate how I feel on the drive to work each day. Unless you can give me some other option, I'll be sitting with the retirement counselor tomorrow morning."

Very sad in that moment, I simply listened. On that afternoon, as we considered Paul's concerns, I didn't have any helpful suggestions. I knew no easy remedy. With me not knowing his "way back home," I just suggested that he might want to sleep on it.

However, I did receive this promise from Paul: "I won't make a final decision until we talk in a couple of days."

How My Own Work Has Been Sustained

As I considered the ways I might assist my friend through his tough times, I surveyed my own lifetime of work. As a school leader, I've taken as my initial task trying to find the true center of a school community, using basic, yet critical questions (now using words given to me by William Stafford): Who are the people? And what are they calling out for? Once I've discovered the community's sense of identity and purpose, I've considered my ongoing work to be energizing the whole school community in the direction of the vision they found profoundly compelling and worthy of their total community effort.

I wondered, "What has sustained me as I've attempted to do that work?" Through times both bad and good, my friends and colleagues have kept me moving in my chosen direction. In truth, I've been very fortunate in terms of the particular friends and acquaintances with whom I've become connected. Roland Barth and I have been friends for approximately twenty-five years. His belief that we "improve schools from within" has constantly sustained me (Barth, 1990). William Stafford came to Alaska to share his poems, but what I received from conversations with him was his caution that I not impose my vision on those with whom I worked. Rather, I was to honor the people with whom I lived. I spent time with Henri Nouwen, and during a visit with him in Toronto, he urged me, "Lose yourself in the work of the group, then find yourself again, energizing the group." In addition, I've felt nourished by my ongoing association with The Harvard Principals' Center and The International Network of Principals' Centers.

These people and organizations encouraged and aided me in my work as a school leader. But one friend has kept me deeply rooted in myself. I believe that I first met Parker Palmer almost twenty-five years ago at Kirkridge, a retreat center in eastern Pennsylvania. There, in the late 1970s, I first heard him talk about how we might turn to issues of the heart as we thought about leadership: "The power of authentic leadership is found not in external arrangements, but in the human heart. Authentic leaders in every setting—from families to nation-states—aim at liberating the heart (their own and others'), so that its powers can liberate the world." On hearing these words, I was certain that I needed to learn more about Palmer's "authentic leadership." This was the sustenance I needed!

The work of Parker Palmer has inspired the establishment of the Center for Teacher Formation and the rationale for Courage to Teach™ and Courage to Lead programs nationwide. (Although any educator can attend either retreat program, typically the Courage to Teach™ programs are oriented toward teachers and the Courage to Lead programs are directed toward school administrators.) Palmer's writings and professional renewal programs have enabled me, time and time again, to return to my true center. Understanding more clearly who I am makes it possible for me to be with others who want to understand themselves better so that they can do their work with a clearer sense of purpose. Feeling more centered myself has made it possible for me to be with educators living in their own tough times. It's one thing to have identified our core values once and quite a different thing to be steadily acting from those beliefs on a day-to-day basis. The press of difficulties in the day-to-day may push us away from the core values that led us to become educators in the first place. I'm convinced that once we stray from the reasons we became educators in the beginning, it's pretty easy to become lost and alone within our professional setting. "Courage work" enables my sustained connection to a sense of myself and to my clear professional purpose.

Typically, Courage to Teach™ or Courage to Lead work is offered in sets of seasonal retreats over a period of one or two years. Participants come together for a two- to three-day period once in autumn, again in winter, once more in spring, and finally in summer. In the context of poems and stories used as prompts (these are referred to as "third things" in Courage work), educators are offered the opportunity to recognize and accept their unique self. They identify their "birthright gifts," reflecting on the talents and special abilities they've brought to a lifetime of work in schools. An example of a third thing is William Stafford's poem "Silver Star" (1996).

Silver Star

To be a mountain you have to climb alone
and accept all that rain and snow. You have to look
far away when evening comes. If a forest
grows, you care; you stand there leaning against
the wind, waiting for someone with faith enough
to ask you to move. Great stones will tumble
against each other and gouge your sides. A storm
will live somewhere in your canyons hoarding its lightning.

If you are lucky, people will give you a dignified
name and bring crowds to admire how sturdy you are,
how long you can hold still for the camera. And some time,
they say, if you last long enough you will hear God;
a voice will roll down from the sky and all your patience
will be rewarded. The whole world will hear it: "Well done."

Using such poems induces us to move out of ourselves for a moment, to see or appreciate something that might not be visible if examined directly.

At the heart of Courage retreat activity is the centuries-old Clearness Committee process. The practice of learning how to ask one another open and honest questions about the significant issues in our lives often yields important results for participants. Each person in a retreat series is given the opportunity to be a "focus person." The focus person brings a difficulty, problem, or "stuck place" to a small group of five to seven persons, who are allowed only to ask attentive questions in a confidential, trusting space. The session lasts two to three hours. These questioners may ask only open and honest questions, questions to which they couldn't possibly know the answer and that do not further the questioner's own agenda or curiosity. Using this ancient Quaker practice, no grandstanding, advice giving, or storytelling on the part of the questioners is allowed. The focus is on the person who has brought the issue or difficulty to the group. Results are rewarding, if not always immediately obvious, often unfolding in the weeks and months that follow. Devotees of this way of being present to our friends and colleagues say, "The Clearness process just goes on and on." Indeed, over the past five years, as I have engaged in the Clearness process and Courage to Teach™ and Courage to Lead retreats with scores of educators, I've observed the Courage process of renewal constantly succeeding. Participants gain clarity; they become more sure of themselves and are able to stand up to difficult situations in schools.

In my experience, it has been this returning to oneself—this finding "home" once more—that has most enabled school leaders to carry on their work during the tough times. Indeed, the challenges that confront school leaders these days are substantial. For one thing, it's not easy to be a school leader as the public watches for school report cards in the press and when schools are closed as a result of such reports. For another, school budgets are strained; difficult choices have to be made. However, I've observed that the school leaders who seem to make it through rough times and who are able to help their school communities to make tough decisions are those who have identified their own core values and who have remained grounded in them while negotiating the core values of the school community. Such school leaders remain steady and at peace with themselves while working with members of their school community, even in difficult times. Yes, these are difficult times indeed. Yet it's possible to live in these tough times when we're steady and at peace with ourselves regarding who we are and why we are doing the work we do.

What Might Work for Paul?

Sadly, my remembering what has sustained me over the years wasn't able to work any overnight magic for Paul. Over dinner that next day, however, I was able to suggest that he put his retirement decision on hold for an entire year. I asked him if he'd ever heard of Parker Palmer. Noticing what appeared to be some genuine interest,

I carefully coaxed him to apply to attend a series of seasonal Courage to Lead retreats. As it turned out, my coaxing wasn't all that necessary. Signing up for the retreats was made a little easier because Paul's best friend, George, also wanted to participate in the retreat series. Both men joined a group that was just forming in a neighboring state. Invited by a team from the Center for Teacher Formation, twenty-five educators from across the state gathered for four weekend retreats over the course of the year. Most of the sessions were held at a retreat center near the center of the state—far enough away from school so that participants felt they were leaving their work behind but close enough for it to be an easy two-hour drive at the end of the work week. They met in November, again in March, once more in May, and, finally, in August.

The group came together that first time in autumn, probably for as many reasons as there were participants. If there was a common theme that brought everyone together on that sparkling fall afternoon, it was probably the desire for professional and personal renewal—renewal of energy, renewal of their mission to make a difference in their workplace, and renewal of their original dedication to education. I invite you now to meet Paul once again, this time as he shared thoughts about his life with others in the retreat setting, season by season.

A Seasonal Journey with Paul

Paul, at the autumn retreat: "I'm an educator, have been for more than twenty years. I am probably what you'd call a teacher-leader. I sort of 'make the school go round.' But, you know, I've run out of steam, and at the same time, I'm about ready to blow my top. One thing you might as well know at the beginning is that I hate administrators. I really do. I loathe them. I know that some of you are the 'them' I loathe. That's okay, and if I don't belong here in the lion's den, you'd better tell me now."

Paul, at the winter retreat: "I'm glad that I'm back with you all. It's not that I'm getting soft on administrators, you understand, because I still hate administrators, but I'm beginning to figure out that you have your problems, too. It's just that I can't figure out why you people don't give those of us who are teacher-leaders a break. Why doesn't my principal give me credit for my work as a morale builder? I bring everybody together in our school, but I'm really quite tired of not being recognized for who I am at my school. I am the informal, and real, 'school head.'"

Paul, at the spring retreat: "Thanks for having me back, you school administrator know-it-alls. It pleases me that some of you are beginning to recognize that a person doesn't have to have the title of a school leader to be one. And I must admit that I'm coming to believe that I wouldn't want to have to deal with some of the crap that you have to deal with just because you have the title 'principal.' In fact, I'm beginning to believe that my school needs both me and the principal in order to have things go well. I'm actually wanting to talk with my principal about all of this as soon as I get back to school this fall."

Paul, at the summer retreat: "You know what I'm going to do when I get home today? I'm having some of my teacher friends over to my apartment for supper. Yes, I cook for my friends. Over supper, I think I'll tell them about how I've mellowed about 'the administration' over the course of this year. I'm beginning to believe that my earlier anger was misdirected. Maybe I wasn't so much angry at you all as I was at myself. Maybe my work life was out of whack, out of balance somehow. Maybe I was, in some way, tired of my teaching and somehow in need of recognition and renewal. Renewal, which, by the way, I've received here over these past few months. You know, as it turns out, I'm really looking forward to the beginning of school. It's just two weeks away now. It's going to be a really good year. And I know that you'll find this pretty hard to believe, but over the past few days I've even given some thought to becoming a principal. I may call some of you next year about that possibility. Thanks!"

Finding Home Once More

As Paul looked back on his time spent with educational leaders in the Courage to Lead retreats, he was amazed at the changes he'd made over the year. So were many others. But Paul wasn't the only person who'd changed. Almost all of the participants had arrived tired and discouraged but ended up feeling enthusiastic and encouraged. Everyone, on saying their good-byes, used the word "revived" or something similar to describe their experience of the year. Paul seemed to speak for everyone when he thanked the group with these words: "I feel such a sense of gratitude. My gratitude is surely directed to the facilitators who invited us here, but just as surely, my feelings of gratitude are directed to all of you. You've made it possible for me to leave here today feeling totally alive and fully charged. I am ready to be with the administrator folks, my school parents, and with all my teacher friends. Students—I'm ready for all who will come my way. Where I was once considering retirement, I'm now in this work for the long haul. I'm so delighted to be my old self again; somehow it feels like I've come home."

Leadership in Tough Times

As I write these words, the principal of the high school just five miles from where I live has announced that he's stepping down. He is quoted in our local paper as saying, "Any more, [school leaders] are simply butchers. We are just butchering up our budgets. All you do is cut, cut, cut—and that's a hard thing when what you want to do is build programs and be able to say that you made a significant contribution."

My guess is that all school leaders want to make a difference as a result of their efforts day to day. Given the context of financial constraints and the intense focus on test scores, these are tough times for school leaders and their school communities. Of course, it's easy to say that we just need to tough it out. For school leaders to have a serious impact, we must facilitate our school communities' articulation of what they most deeply care about for their young people and for themselves. Even in the toughest of times, connecting people more tightly to their genuine hopes and dreams is possible. It becomes absolutely possible when leaders are centered, steady, and secure in themselves. Our way back home to everything we want for our children and ourselves is to be found when we are tough with ourselves about those things that are genuinely important to us. In tough times, we must stand up and speak out for what's truly in our hearts. Indeed, what's truly in our hearts for the common good can, as Parker Palmer suggests, "liberate the world."

Chapter Nineteen

What Is Expected of Us?

"We've come to listen to your heart." So announced the cardiologists as they entered the hospital room following my heart surgery. "First, we'll listen for the beat and the rhythm. Then we'll want to listen for your heart's voice. In other words, we'll want to hear about your heart from you."

As they placed the stethoscope on my chest, I tried to puzzle out what these physicians had just said to me. Of course, I understood their need to listen for the strength and regularity of my heart. But wanting to hear about my heart from me—I didn't get that part at all! "What is expected of me?" That was the question that tumbled out of my mouth in the hospital room that morning. "What is expected of me in terms of your wanting to hear from me about my heart? Just what is it that you want to know?"

The surgeons exchanged glances, and then my coordinating cardiologist explained in a matter of fact way: "We just want to hear the words that come from your heart today. We don't want to learn from you about your thoughts; rather, if your heart spoke to us this morning, what would it say? We just want to hear your heart's voice."

On my bedside table rested the poem "Epitaph" by Merritt Malloy, from Wayne Muller's *How, Then, Shall We Live? Four Simple Questions That Reveal the Beauty and Meaning of Our Lives* (1997). Since I truly believed that death was close upon me, and I thought this was coming from my heart, I simply read my physicians this poem:

When I die,
give what's left of me to children
and old men that wait to die.
And if you need to cry,
cry for your brother walking the street
beside you.
When you need me,
put your arms around anyone
and give them what you need to give to me.

I want to leave you something,
something better than words or sounds:
look for me in the people I've known
or loved.
And if you cannot give me away,
at least let me live in your eyes
and not on your mind.
You can love me most
by letting hands touch hands,
by letting bodies touch bodies,
and by letting go of children
that need to be free.

Love doesn't die; people do.
So that when all that's left of me is love,
give me away.
I'll see you at home in the earth.

On hearing the poem, the physicians nodded approvingly and left.

Soon I left the hospital and commenced the healing process at home. As the days went by, I discovered that my earlier fears of death were, to say the least, premature. With medication and the needed physical health routines, I was proceeding nicely with my "recovered life." I was making great progress; in fact, I was beginning to feel pretty much like my old self. Life was certainly looking up!

One month later, I found myself on an elevator at the hospital, suddenly surrounded by four members of my cardiology team. It was noontime, and apparently they had just finished up their morning surgery routine. I was on my way home from an X-ray checkup of my chest when they happened on me. My cardiologist pulled out his stethoscope—right there in the elevator, mind you—and said to me, "I'm going to listen to your heart, David. I need to listen for the rhythm." After he did that, he called out, much more loudly than is allowed for elevator talk, "Now, David, what do you know about your heart's voice this afternoon?"

Well, it just so happened that I had been reading a children's book in the X-ray waiting room. So, right there in the elevator, I read (with rather profound embarrassment) to these doctors of mine—and to four other members of the elevator audience—words about how we need to listen to and trust the voice that speaks inside of us, letting us know what is right and wrong for us.

One of the physicians, standing in the absolute center of the elevator, called out, "I know those words; they're from Shel Silverstein's book *Falling Up*. I read those words to my kids last night. That's pretty interesting stuff. My kids understood what he was getting at, and it sounds like you do too, David. I can't wait to see what you bring to us at your checkup in July!"

As the door opened and my companions departed, I breathed a sigh of relief and thought, "Just what have I gotten myself into here?"

My July checkup came around all too quickly, not because I was fearful about the physical test results but because I was wondering what exam room poetry would best describe my heart's voice at this time. I had figured out my cardiology team's modus operandi, and it was actually beginning to make sense to me. They knew that a person's physical health was influenced greatly by their heartfelt attitudes. So I was spending time between visits with them determining just the perfect readings from my heart.

Sure enough, as expected, they greeted me that July with "It's great to see you, David. First, we're going to listen for the rhythm and the beat, and then we'll ask for your report. As you've come to expect, we'll want to hear your heart's voice."

Well, for weeks—not simply in anticipation of the exam, but because my heart felt so full and ready for a new and different life— I'd been walking around Portland with a copy of Mary Oliver's poem, "The Summer Day," (1990) in my pocket. So I was thoroughly prepared to read these words:

> *Who made the world?*
> *Who made the swan, and the black bear?*
> *Who made the grasshopper?*
> *This grasshopper, I mean—*
> *the one who has flung herself out of the grass,*
> *the one who is eating sugar out of my hand,*
> *who is moving her jaws back and forth instead of up and down—*
> *who is gazing around with her enormous and complicated eyes.*
> *Now she lifts her pale forearms and thoroughly washes her face.*
> *Now she snaps her wings open, and floats away.*
> *I don't know exactly what a prayer is.*
> *I do know how to pay attention, how to fall down*
> *into the grass, how to kneel down in the grass,*
> *how to be idle and blessed, how to stroll through the fields,*
> *which is what I have been doing all day.*
> *Tell me, what else should I have done?*
> *Doesn't everything die at last, and too soon?*
> *Tell me, what is it you plan to do*
> *with your one wild and precious life?*

I told the little group that the reason I'd selected this reading for my July checkup was that my heart's voice was much more relaxed and optimistic now. They assured me that they believed that this was true for me, and I thought that this remark would be their good-bye.

But just as I was placing my copy of the poem back in my pocket, one of the physicians let me know that they had a few extra minutes that day and that during those few minutes, they wanted to talk with me about the "implications and ramifications of listening to, and speaking with, one's heart's voice." Specifically, since they knew I was involved with school leadership, they wanted to talk about what "listening to and speaking from the heart had to do with life in organizations."

"Aha," I thought, "these folks know me well." At this point, it really clicked: "These guys truly care about me!" I thought. "Something very special is going on here with my cardiological 'heart's voice' team."

During the conversation that followed, the members of my team congratulated me on my speedy recovery. They shared with me the possibility that my body knowledge (how I knew my body), combined with my willingness to speak with my heart's voice, spelled a "bright future indeed" for me. Then we all went on to consider the question that, apparently, they'd often asked themselves: What might happen in organizations if all of the participants spoke with their heart's voices? (At this point, I wondered whether they might be interested in speaking from the heart about what it felt like to work in organizations ruled by insurance guidelines.) For my part, I said that organizations would be more like genuine communities if all their members spoke their truths straight from the heart. They all nodded knowingly, and then, unfortunately, as is wont to happen in medical settings, they were called off to some emergency.

In the time since this "heart experience," I've often thought of how things might have been different in the schools I'd known if only I had pleaded with everyone to speak from the heart. Of course, speaking from the heart challenges most of us! The personal work of finding that voice in each of us can be difficult, and it can take time.

However, because of what I learned from my cardiology team, I now understand that in schools, as in all areas of life, what is expected of us is to speak with our heart's voice. In fact, that truth set me to writing this book. Speaking from the heart always requires us to be vulnerable. During one of my conversations with Henri Nouwen, the renowned theologian, he challenged me. Henri dared me, as part of my work as a principal, to "be totally vulnerable" and to "share my every hope, fear, and concern" with the staff. "I'll guarantee you," Henri went on to say, "that your honesty will bring forth their honesty, and the very nature, the everyday climate, of your school will change. If you want to create leaders in your school community, speaking from your heart will get you to your goal sooner than any other way." Speaking with the heart's voice is the kind of communication among staff and by the principal that makes possible the creation of a community of leaders, keen on learning. As I think back on my work at Denali School, I know that I often felt vulnerable and tried to speak from that place. Others did, too. Perhaps what happened occurred because we tried to speak from the heart.

Chapter Twenty

What Do You Do for Your Living?

In April 2000, I experienced a "heart event," as you've read in the previous story. In the months following my cardiovascular surgery, a physician friend offered me an experience that illuminated my life and helped me determine my future. Actually, it allowed me to re-examine my life, and it gave me perspective on it.

My physician friend had married a woman from France. He practiced medicine in the United States, but they maintained a family home in France. Just six weeks into my recovery, he suggested that their farmhouse in Provence might be a perfect place to continue my healing process. "It's pretty basic," my physician friend cautioned. "The house is a hundred-year-old stone building in the middle of a vineyard, and it's about two miles from town." He went on to declare, "They'll be harvesting the grapes when you'll be there, and I think it would be a fascinating time for you to be in the south of France. In my opinion, the farmhouse and surrounding fields could provide just the kind of healing that you most need." Then he volunteered, "You could be harvesting your life stories inside the house while they're harvesting grapes just outside the door."

As it turned out, this little book resulted from my friend's invitation to visit his farmhouse near Cotignac, France. I did harvest my life stories during the two months amid the vineyards. But something else happened there, too. I met Marcel.

My wife, Karen, and I found our first days at the farmhouse nothing less than spellbinding. The *vendange*, the grape harvest, was just beginning when we arrived. I watched through our window for the first couple of days. Later, I placed a chair at the edge of the field. I watched the grapes being picked by hand and by a gigantic machine. The process went on, day after day. For a week or so, I sat there, engaged and intrigued. As time went on, it became clear to me that the fellow in charge of the *vendange*, at least on this piece of land, was Marcel, the fellow my physician friend had mentioned before I'd left Oregon. Observing from the edge of the field, I watched this French farm fellow harvesting the grapes, row after row.

After a couple of weeks, I decided that it was time to get out my camera and capture some of this experience for friends and family back home. Approaching this fellow I'd been observing for days, I asked, "Photo, OK, Marcel?" I was such a know-nothing when it came to speaking French that I just gestured at my camera and then at him. "Photo, OK, Marcel?" I must have called out these words stupidly for a good minute or two. And then I noticed that Marcel was smiling.

"Of course you may take my picture, David. Do you want me out among the plants or up on my machine?" Stunned, I blurted out, "Oh, up on the machine, but how is it that you know my name?"

Simply amazed to hear the crystal-clear words coming my way in English, I was all the more shocked to hear him continue: "Well, I know your name, just like you know mine, and I know a few things about you."

Marcel went on, "However, I don't know the answer to an important question: What do you do for your living?"

I told him that I was a college professor. He snickered a little and went on, "Oh, no, I didn't mean that. I want to know how you live."

Speechless, I just stood there. When I finally found my voice again, I told Marcel how much I was enjoying my time in France and in that part of Provence. Marcel began to tell me about traditions in this part of Provence; he smiled and asked, "Have you found your *santon?*

Santon? "Well, uh, no; what is a *santon?*" I looked up at Marcel perched on his big green harvesting machine, and after a moment's quiet, he taught me about *santons*. He told me that *santons* originated in Provence as figures for the Christmas crèche and that because the crèche scene was surrounded by a larger village setting in many three-dimensional depictions, some *santons* came to reflect the people in a traditional village and the jobs they filled. These painted clay figures were dressed to represent ordinary people; one might be a gardener, another a cook, one a priest, a fisherman, a blacksmith, or the mayor. Marcel concluded, "But to me and my friends, we think there's more to *santons* than simply figurines that are used as a part of the Christmas celebration." Marcel became quite animated when he shared, "To me, a *santon* represents the truth about my life. I believe that a *santon* shows who I am in my heart. Do you understand what I mean, David?"

When I responded that I did understand and appreciated his words, Marcel pointed to the southeast and urged, "Go to the town of Nice, David, and look around the shops there. Along the side streets, you'll find a number of shops that carry *santons*. You'll find hundreds of them. I'd like you to very carefully choose your *santon*. Remember, the question I asked you was What do you do for your living? I want you to live with this question, select your *santon*, be with your *santon* for a year or so, and then come back to tell me how it's been, living with your *santon*. When you return, be prepared to fully respond to my important question: What do you do for your living?"

In a week or so, Karen and I went to Nice. I checked out the shops. Since I typically hate to go shopping, I'm sure that Karen was amazed that I spent so much time going from store to store. I was truly on a mission and on a rather difficult one at that. Who am I really? Who am I in my heart? How do I live? Weren't those the questions that Marcel wanted me to live with as I looked at *santon* after *santon*?

"How can I possibly find some little figure that represents what it is that I do for my living?" I thought. It was a daunting task. Over the morning hours of that day, I just couldn't figure things out. But

I carefully looked and looked at the representations I was shown. I saw one of a gardener and thought, "Maybe this is the one, because I 'make the desert places green.'"

Then I saw a storyteller, and I mused, "I do tell stories, and I encourage others to tell stories about their lives. Maybe this is the one."

Finally, my eyes fell upon this lamplighter guy. I stood before him for just the longest time. "Are you *me?*" I said these words very quietly, almost in a kind of hush. I looked and looked. And then I noticed that, in addition to the lamp he carried, there was an umbrella.

Perhaps it was the umbrella that decided things for me. I live in Portland, Oregon, where it rains a lot. But in addition to that, the lamp and umbrella do represent what I do for my living. I hold up a light so that others can find their way. And I'm there for others in their stormy times. "Maybe," I thought, "this lamplighter guy is me."

Well, I've been living with the lamplighter guy on my writing desk for three years now, and soon I will return to France. I'm beginning to work out the words that I'll share with Marcel in answer to the question he asked: What do you do for your living?

My response to his question might go something like this: I've heard writing described as being like walking through a dark room with a lantern, which illuminates the things that were always there. That saying also pretty well describes my experience of writing stories about leadership when I was at that Provençal farmhouse three years ago. It also recounts the experience of living with my chosen *santon.* Although I struggle with life, as we all do, I have always been there, simply holding the lamp for others. I've held up that lamp so that they might see their own way. I've evoked, energized, and encouraged.

So perhaps, Marcel, this is my answer to your question. What I do for my living is to hold up a lantern for others in my community, not so much to "shed light" in the sense of providing meaning to their situation as to "give light" so that what is already there can be seen and so that people can find their way. Doing so contributes to the creation of community. This is what I tried to do at Denali School.

Yes, Marcel, living with my *santon* has helped me make sense of my life. It's also helped me understand more fully how to create a sense of community in schools. Thanks!

Part Four

Making a Difference

The phrase "pay it forward" relates to a concept about making a difference. While the movie built on the idea may not have made great waves in many circles, the idea of doing something for another person for whom it would make an important difference, without the need to be paid back by that individual, serves as a powerful lesson in our self-centered times. Giving when we don't know the outcome or expect a reward takes faith in abundance.

The arena in which I've tried to make a difference with my professional life—tried to "pay it forward"—has been in the realm of school leadership. Professionally, my life's work has been either serving as a principal or working to prepare principals. As you've read, many people—most especially those at Denali School—have energized and encouraged me in my work and in my efforts, conscious and unconscious, to contribute my gifts and talents to meeting the world's needs.

Part Four is my invitation to you to make a difference in the world—your world—with your professional life, just as Dean Fritzmeier from my high school days (Chapter Twenty-Two) and the Denali school community (Chapter Twenty-Three) made a difference in mine. If you accept the invitation, I know you'll do it in your own way, appropriate to the people you work with and the characteristics of your community. Keep William Stafford's potent questions close to you: Who are the people you work with? What are they calling out for? Certainly, no two schools are alike, and I haven't told you these stories so that you'll replicate exactly the steps we took at Denali School. Still, I will lay out for you in the next chapter a sketch of the elements that I believe most influenced the unfolding of the Denali Project. Perhaps these elements will inspire the emergence of a vision and a plan that are right for you and your school community. Indeed, if you genuinely "honor the people," who knows where you'll all be led? It depends on how the gifts, interests, passions, concerns, and resources of your community blend with your own. This is the adventure. This is the abundance. This is how you'll make a difference.

Chapter Twenty-One

How to Build a Community of Leaders in Our Schools

In the early 1990s, I was a candidate for superintendent of schools in Sitka, Alaska, but I lost to a candidate with a lot more experience as a superintendent. As I was preparing to board an airplane on being informed of the decision, one of the school board members came up to me and asked, "Want to know why I voted against you?"

"Sure," I said, with a rather surprised look.

"Well, I'm a fisherman. I know that I have visions while I'm out at sea. But I know for sure that a person should not have visions on land."

Perhaps that school board member thought that visions come when one has his or her head in the clouds, when a person is disoriented or has time on their hands. Or maybe he wanted a superintendent who would come with answers and would "get in there and make things happen."

Indeed, I have had visions on land. But my visions relate to a way of being together as a school community, not to making happen a particular image I've brought in for a school or district. I've carried a passion for having all the people who share a connection to a school and its children gather around the work of finding what's right for them. For all of my life, I've disliked so-called leaders who have imposed their will—their notion about what's right—on the people. I'm almost seventy years old now, and for almost all of those years, I have observed leadership bullies and administrator know-it-alls in action. In my work over the years, I've tried to provide another way.

I've illustrated "another way" in the stories I've shared on these pages. Each story has a message. Each story provides hints and clues toward a vital, meaningful, connected, effective, refreshing way to conceive of and accomplish the work of school leadership. I've tried to suggest that leaders go the extra mile to reach out to the people (sometimes literally, as in "Walking Them Home" and "Blue Bicycle Summer"), that leaders find out what people are passionate about and foster the connection of those interests to the school's vision for itself (as in the ice rink story in Chapter Four), that leaders energize the members of the school community to learn something new together (as in the stories about the Friday School in Chapters Two, Three, and Five), that leaders encourage meaningful ways for members of the school community to work together (as in "Karaoke Homecoming"), and that leaders speak from the heart (as in "What Is Expected of Us?"). More than anything, overall, and in every imaginable fashion, I've tried to suggest ways that school leaders can honor the people. It's this spirit that I hope infused and informed all the elements of the Denali Project and my interpretation of it through these stories. It's this spirit that brought forth our experience of abundance. It's this spirit that must animate your adaptation of the elements that I am about to summarize, should you elect to incorporate them into your own school community's story. I offer them for your consideration as a thumbnail sketch, not as a recipe or a list of dos and don'ts. I address my remarks to principals, but of course these concepts can be applied by everyone in the school community.

The creation of a community of leaders in any school requires, first and foremost, an attitude of servanthood on the part of the principal. The principal brings an attitude of service to all the important tasks of that role—for example, ensuring the safety and well-being of the children or building an excellent school program for the learning of children and adults. This attitude may take the principal months or even years to develop. In order to serve the school community well, the principal needs to find out what people associated with the school are passionate about and then pour it on. The principal's responsibility is to evoke and identify the assets and strengths of the school community and then to find ways to promote, support, energize, and encourage the individual gifts and talents that have been identified—whether the school leader is focused on the young people, the teacher, or the parents. Furthermore, if it's your goal to create a community of leaders, you need to understand that laying the foundation for an organization of that sort requires doing some grunt work. Whether it's delivering teacher assignments on a bicycle or helping out with secretarial duties in the school office, no task is too menial. No task should be considered beneath your station in life. Accepting the responsibility to serve is the first step toward building a community of leaders in your school.

Once you accept an attitude of service and the behavior to match, it's time to ask your version of the question I stumbled onto: What do you want for your children, here at this school? Ask that question in various forms of everyone connected with the school community. Of the children, ask, "What do you really want to learn while you're a student here? And how do you want to learn it?" Of the teachers, inquire, "What do you truly want for the young people you serve?" Of the parents, query, "All things considered, what hopes do you hold for your children and how might this school nurture what you hope for them?" In all these (and other) myriad ways, ask the key question month after month. Ask that question one on one, in small hallway conversations, and in large-group situations. Keep asking the question until the answers begin to come together. That's another element toward creating a community of leaders in your school.

The third element can be the most exciting and fun part of the community-building process. Once the members of the school community have declared and shaped the purpose of their school, they identify what needs to be learned in order to support their vision. It's important that everyone learn something brand-new, something that none of you knew before. The principal must be a co-learner. At the same time, you have talent and expertise in your school community that could be of immense benefit in helping your school community advance its learning. It's critical that teachers and parents, in meeting the school community's request to share their knowledge, also adopt a stance of service and servanthood. If anyone thinks that he or she possesses expert status, the hierarchy that's produced by such thinking undermines the process of letting go that is necessary for real learning to occur. You become a learning community centered on a need or a skill you have identified that's essential to the creation of the school you all want. You do that learning together. You become like little kids again. And in the process, you become an energized community.

Coincidental to the process of becoming a learning community, individuals are likely to step forward to offer their unique talents and skills for the good of the overall organization. This is the initial emergence of the group becoming the leader, a fourth element in the establishment of a community of leaders. If such leadership is not evolving, consider encouraging it by directly asking individuals which aspects of the developing project they'd like to become involved with and which talents and gifts of theirs they feel might fit. If quite a few key staff members, parents, or organizations are not connecting and contributing to the project, it may be a clue to you that the discussion and framing of the school's intents and purposes hasn't gone deep enough to get at the school community's true vision, its true answer to the question "What do you want for your children, here at this school?" When the school community finds its true vision, everyone is rewarded with seeing one another voluntarily, willingly, even enthusiastically and lovingly offering their unique talents and gifts to the organization that they've come to value.

Lose yourself in the work of the group. That's the fifth element in the process. Give yourself over completely to whatever your school community has identified as the major work to be done, whether or not it fits your particular background or expertise. Yes, lose yourself in that work, and find yourself again, energizing the people for the work that's to be done. This part can be fun, too, if you are willing and able to let go and trust the school's purposes and people while periodically asking everyone to check in with the school community's vision. I think that you'll find yourself saying, "Now this is why I decided to become a school principal in the first place!"

You'll flow with the process of community building beyond the point of no return. Really, there will be no turning back. You'll be beyond worrying about high-stakes testing. You'll be beyond wondering what your fellow principals think of what you're doing. You'll be way beyond worrying whether you're going to make it to retirement. Truthfully, you'll be beyond yourself. That is, in the most fundamental sense, you'll have forgotten thoughts and concerns about yourself. Sure, there will be moments when you will want to consider your own needs and concerns, but mainly you'll find yourself caught up in the focus and excitement of creating the optimal learning community for everyone you were hired to serve. I honestly believe that you will be having the time of your life.

Having lost yourself (in the best sense), it's possible to lead outrageously—that is, to take steps you couldn't have imagined yourself dreaming up or accomplishing. I speak of living and leading with boldness, but it's a boldness that arrives through humility.

The Denali Project called for boldness, a kind of boldness that comes from standing up to prevailing cultural attitudes of looking for deficits and focusing on scarcity thinking. At the present time, we read and hear only about what schools and teachers, children and their families are lacking—how they are not performing well, how values are absent. Of course, education budgets do suffer, programs are cut, class sizes increase; too many poor children and children of color do not receive the education they deserve; teachers are maligned. We need to recognize such challenges and work to strengthen public support for public education. Nevertheless, focusing on deficits rather than emphasizing assets, believing that there's never enough while holding tightly to "what's mine" causes us to abandon our highest values and purposes. We get caught up in fear; we lose sight of who we are and who we can become.

In these times, we need to take a look at educational concerns from a different angle. This book tells an inspiring story of abundance—a story about what a school community understood about itself and the ways that community members created the school they wanted for their children and themselves. I invite you to honor the people in your school community, live with an attitude of abundance, and in so doing, build a community of leaders.

Chapter Twenty-Two

My Thank You to the Dean

For all of my work life, I've wanted to "make a difference." Fifty years ago, I received a gift that might just explain why.

I was a senior in a Chicago-area high school, planning a school-to-work transition that involved getting a job in the building trades, perhaps as a cabinetmaker. Many members of my family were painters and carpenters, and I was planning to join them in some way. I wanted to work with my hands.

I was looking forward to such work, when the school's dean of senior boys, Mr. Fritzmeier, surprised me by asking, "What are your plans for college, David?"

Rather stunned, I explained: "I'm not going to college. No one in our family has ever gone to college; we don't have much money at home, and I'm really looking forward to going into carpentry work."

The dean, studying me, announced, "We'll see about that. Meet me in my office tomorrow at this exact same time. Understand?"

I assured him, "Yes, tomorrow, at the same time."

The next day, the dean asked, "David, do you have anything planned for this weekend?"

Trying to recall any arranged hot dates or scheduled alley games of basketball, I realized there was nothing. "No big plans," I responded.

"Good," he said with a smile. "Be here Friday at one o'clock, bag packed for the weekend. Don't worry; just know that the two days you'll be away will be life-changing."

When Friday came, the dean drove me downtown to Chicago's Rock Island railroad station. He informed me, "You're traveling to Grinnell College, and when you get there, someone will meet you. Here are your tickets. As the miles go by, rejoice in the adventure of it all, knowing that you're appreciated. And one more thing: be prepared to enthusiastically say, 'Yes, of course.'"

On my arrival at the Grinnell train station, I was greeted and taken to a dorm room to settle in. For the next day and a half, I sat in on Saturday classes, attended a dance, and talked with what seemed like the entire college community. Upon leaving the college on Sunday, I heard from the admissions staff: "Expect to hear from us soon, David; you'll probably be invited to be with us here at Grinnell. For now, we can say that someone has arranged to have your college expenses taken care of for you. So, would you like to attend Grinnell?"

As Mr. Fritzmeier directed, I offered my enthusiastic "Yes, of course."

Years later, I learned that the dean had paid for that train trip, and, from what I have been able to figure out, he made possible my four years at Grinnell. Perhaps he arranged for my work-study and other financial aid. Maybe he paid something out of his own pocket. I just don't know. In a conversation with him about all this many years later, he revealed, "Your Grinnell gift was simply about my wanting to make a difference in the life of at least one person in my lifetime. By way of thanks, promise me that you'll try to do the same, knowing all the while that you may never know for sure whether you've made that difference. Just keep trying; watch for your chances with each new day."

I promised Mr. Fritzmeier that I'd do the same. I tried to make a difference at Denali Elementary. I continue to watch for my chances. It's my thank you to the dean.

Chapter Twenty-Three

At the Intersection of Innocence and Wisdom

One of the things I see more clearly now that I've been away from my Denali experience for a number of years is the utmost importance of that moment in the dark hallway when I asked the question "What do you want for your children, here at Denali School?" Now, viewing that question from a distance of many years, I realize that unconsciously, I had dropped all pretense of knowing anything. I was no longer trying to use graduate school knowledge to give the right answers about what to do. I had moved into a precious arena of pure innocence, innocence in the sense of both "lack of knowledge" and "purity of heart." Since I didn't have a clue about what I was doing, I stumbled into what became a most intriguing and powerful question for our school community. On one hand, my innocence at that moment made an incredible, potent conversation possible. On the other hand, I am now also wondering if there was, in the midst of that individually innocent moment, some form of collective wisdom at work as well? Was I—were we—at the intersection of innocence and wisdom during those minutes in the hallway? I believe we were, just as I now believe that the phrase "living and working at the intersection of innocence and wisdom" aptly describes the Denali school community when I knew it best.

At this intersection of innocence and wisdom, and in the course of my daily and monthly activities at the school, the Denali community called me back home to myself and to my vocation, as well as offered me new understandings and gifts. Maybe before I came to Denali School, I had lost track of who I was and my deepest purposes in my educational work. That community helped me to remember. This poem, "Calling" by Daniel Hong-Soo Kim, which I heard at a Systems Thinking in Action conference in 1996, explains what the Denali people did for me.

> *You call my name*
> *long after it has been forgotten*
> *by all who say they love me.*
>
> *You touch me*
> *at the core of my being*
> *while others have left,*
> *believing that there is nothing there.*
>
> *You breathe love*
> *into the vessel of my heart*
> *and fill it with warmth and tenderness*
> *even as others take from me*
> *my last*
> *gasping*
> *breath.*
>
> *You hold me in a sacred space,*
> *honoring me for who I am,*
> *while others honor me*
> *for who they want me to be.*
>
> *You call my name,*
> *and I am moved to tears*
> *because I too had forgotten.*

Among storytellers (and, apparently, poets too) there's a line that goes like this: Any sorrow can be borne, if we but tell it in a story (or a poem). My sorrow was, and is, that I left the school that captured my heart. Earlier in these pages, I wrote about "a people far from home" and how the experience of creating a learning community at Denali School brought these people home. Well, if the truth be told, the experiences shared in the stories you have now read brought me home as well. To all of you who continue to call the Denali family your home, either literally or figuratively, I say thank you for taking me in and teaching me about my life and work. Most especially, I thank you for teaching me what is not typically learned in graduate school. You taught me that a school community is quite willing to put up with, even embrace, what might seem outrageous, provided it is all focused on what is best for the children. Thanks for letting me offer my own gifts and talents as you offered yours abundantly. In the process, you deepened my understanding of school leadership and how to build a community of leaders, a community that loves to learn. More than anything, you taught me the significance of the word *honor*. Actually, you taught me that if we do nothing else but honor one another, we are doing well. You taught me to honor the past and to trust the future. You taught me to like myself and to love you. I miss you. I care about you. I wish you well.

Afterword: Knowing Why
We're Doing the Work

Everyone leaned in toward one another around the small table, and at that moment, I knew yet another reason that I'd been doing my life's work in the way that I'd been doing it. Just prior to the publication of this book, I visited members of my family in Kållered, Sweden. There I found the life that I had known as a young boy growing up in Swedish America (as I called it at the time), still going on. My relatives on Sweden's west coast live in homes that are cozily clustered together. When I was a child in the American Midwest, all of my grandparents, aunts, uncles, and cousins lived no more than a twenty-minute walk from my home. Often our entire family would crowd together around my grandmother's dining room table. Gathered around that table, we were then, as my family in Sweden is now, very eager to hear about one another's adventures and desires. Our way of listening to one another, then and now, is strongly characteristic of our family. It's a deep listening that has fostered a love of simply being together; it supports and encourages us in our day-to-day living.

It is now clear to me that throughout my lifetime as a school leader trying to build community, I was building on these ways of being a family, these ways I had known as a child. As a school principal, often living among persons who expressed concerns about being far from home, I just did what came naturally to me. Believing as I did in the value of a supportive family, I invited and coaxed everyone into a working community where they felt they belonged.

I learned to do the work of community building from my family. I've been making this effort in schools throughout my years

171

because I believe that we all learn better when we are living and working within a family forum than we do in groups that are formed into organizations. I've been doing my work in this way because I want others to experience the joy that I did by being among people who are accepting and encouraging and eager to listen and to learn.

How about you? Why are you doing your work? Perhaps knowing who you are will help you know why you're doing your work, and knowing both will help you bring significant benefits to your school community. I leave you then with these wishes: May you know yourself well; may you know and honor the persons in your community and the passions they seek to embody; may you envision good work together; may your school be more like family.

Sisters, Oregon   DAVID HAGSTROM
February 2004

References

Barth, R. S. *Improving Schools from Within: Teachers, Parents, and Principals Can Make a Difference*. San Francisco: Jossey-Bass, 1990.

Greenleaf, R. *Servant Leadership: A Journey into the Nature of Legitimate Power and Greatness*. New York: Paulist Press, 1977.

Hagstrom, D. "A People Far from Home." *Chicago Tribune*, Sept. 26, 1981, Perspective section, p. 1.

Heider, J. *The Tao of Leadership: Leadership Strategies for a New Age*. New York: Bantam Books, 1986.

Jaworski, J. *Synchronicity: The Inner Path of Leadership*. San Francisco: Berrett-Koehler, 1996.

Kim, D. "Calling." Unpublished poem presented at the Systems Thinking in Action Conference, San Francisco, 1996.

Little, J. W. "Norms of Collegiality and Experimentation: Workplace Conditions of School Success." *American Educational Research Journal*, 1982, *19*(3), 325–340.

Lockwood, A. T. "Forging a New Frontier." *Focus in Change*, Fall 1991, pp. 11–13. (Published by the National Center for Effective Schools Research and Development.)

Muller, W. *How, Then, Shall We Live? Four Simple Questions That Reveal the Beauty and Meaning of Our Lives*. New York: Bantam Books, 1997.

Oliver, M. "The Summer Day." In M. Oliver, *House of Light*. Boston: Beacon Press, 1990.

O'Neil, J. "On Schools as Learning Organizations: A Conversation with Peter Senge." *Educational Leadership*, Apr. 1995, *52*(7), 20–23.

Palmer, P. J. *The Courage to Teach: Exploring the Inner Landscape of a Teacher's Life*. San Francisco: Jossey-Bass, 1998.

Palmer, P. J. *Let Your Life Speak: Listening for the Voice of Vocation*. San Francisco: Jossey-Bass, 2000.

Peck, M. S. *The Different Drum: Community Making and Peace*. New York: Simon & Schuster, 1987.

Pipher, M. *The Shelter of Each Other: Rebuilding Our Families*. New York: Putnam, 1996.

Pomeroy, D. "Beliefs into Practice: An Exploration of Linkage Between Elementary Teachers' Beliefs About the Nature of Science and Their Classroom Practices." Unpublished doctoral dissertation, Graduate School of Education, Harvard University, 1993.

Silverstein, S. *Falling Up*. New York: HarperCollins, 1996.

Stafford, W. "Silver Star." In W. Stafford, *Even in Quiet Places*. Lewiston, Idaho: Confluence Press, 1996.

Stafford, W. "The Way It Is." In W. Stafford, *The Way It Is: New & Selected Poems*. St. Paul, Minn.: Graywolf Press, 1998.

Index